MELCHIZEDEK ORDER, THE MATURED PRIESTHOOD

(Outlined Notes by Donald Peart)

Melchizedek Order, the Matured Priesthood© Outlined Notes by Donald Peart

All Scriptural references are:

King James Version ("Public Domain"), unless others wise noted.

All bold text and literal parenthetical phrases in the Scripture references are added by the author for clarity. Single quotes are also used in some texts to highlight a literal definition of the original texts. Hyphens are also used in translation to demonstrate that the translation came from a compound Greek word. Some of the "thee," "thou," "ye," etcetera used in Old English are revised to reflect the modern "you," and so on.

Dictionary reference includes but is not limited to, Strong's Concordance, BibleWorks Software, and ISA2 Basic Software

These outlined notes herein are by no means exhaustive. Also, since most of this book is in outlined form, the scripture references are listed and then notes related to them are discussed below each referenced scripture.

There are also audio teachings on most of the topics in this book that can be provided via email and can be accessed via Google Drive. My contact information is in the back of the book.

Cover design by Donald Peart Jr.

Revised edition using more complete sentences in the notes.

ISBN: 978-1-966856-13-9

OUTLINED CONTENTS

OTHER BOOKS

CONTACT INFORMATION

ABOUT THE AUTHOR:

MELCHIZEDEK ORDER, INTRODUCTION

Jesus is our High Priest according to the order of Melchizedek. This truth is established and explained by the writer of the book of Hebrews. The doctrine concerning Jesus' high priesthood being according to the order of Melchizedek is exceedingly difficult to interpret if the believer is lazy of hearing or immature in discerning between good and bad. However, even though, the "more excellent ministry" of the Lord Jesus' Melchizedek order is difficult to understand and difficult to teach. It does not mean that we should not start the process of learning of the "mature" Melchizedek priesthood the Lord expects His Body of priests <u>to function</u> as, now in this life and the life that is about to come. There is a *Melchizedek Order, the Matured Priesthood* of our Lord Jesus Christ!

Hebrews 5 Introduction
In **Hebrews, chapter 5,** the Melchizedek ministry, as it relates to Jesus, is introduced as the High Priest called of God according to the order of Melchizedek. In **Hebrews, chapter 5,** our Lord Jesus is introduced again as the author of eternal salvation according to the order of Melchizedek. It can also be understood, according to the scriptures, that Melchizedek was first introduced in **Genesis 14,** some four thousand years ago. He is still alive in heaven today, just as our Lord Jesus, **the Highest Priest,** is alive in us and in the heavens.

Hebrews 6 Introduction
In **Hebrews chapter 6,** we see the Lord Jesus as our High-Priest, the Forerunner, into the Holy of Holies, behind the veil of the Temple in heaven, "into the age according to the

order of Melchizedek." In this reference of Melchizedek in **Hebrews chapter 6,** we are to "flee for refuge" behind the veil (representative of one of the cities of refuge) to take refuge with our "Apostle and High-Priest, Jesus Christ." And the Lord Jesus as our High Priest who died and was resurrected eternally "has delivered us," "is delivering us, and "shall yet deliver"[1] us from the avenger of death. He give us a hope concerning God's promises (plural) which are immutable.

Hebrews 7 Introduction

In **Hebrew chapter 7**, the author of the book of Hebrews waded into the difficult interpretation of the Melchizedek order relative to the Lord Jesus Christ and his corporate royal priesthood. We see Melchizedek as Jesus, the King of Righteous-togetherness; Jesus, the King of peace; Jesus, the King of Salem (New Jerusalem), Jesus, the Son of the Highest God, Jesus, who lives eternally through God's oath, Jesus and his priesthood who receives tithe from their brothers, Jesus, the Lawgiver, Jesus having the indestructible life, Jesus, our Intercessor, Jesus as High Priest forever.

Hebrews 8 Introduction

In **Hebrews chapter 8**, the author of book of Hebrews, sums up Jesus' Melchizedek order as our Hight Priest in the right hand of God in the heavens and High Priest over His House in the earth simultaneously. From, **Hebrews 8,** we will also develop the "Great-togetherness" in the heavens. The principles of the New Covenant according to the order of Melchizedek is also clearly explained in the book of **Hebrews chapter 8.** The heavenly father now places and writes his laws in our hearts and deep thoughts. Through the sacrifice

---

[1] Compare 2 Cor 1:10, Heb 5:6-8

of Jesus and the blood of Jesus, once we are forgiven our sins, God does not remember our sins. Through the one sacrifice of our Lord Jesus Christ, there is also no more need for any animal sacrifices forever!

Hebrews 9 Introduction

The interpretation of the order of Melchizedek relative to the better blood of Jesus purifying our consciences are also developed in **Hebrews chapter 9** and **Hebrews chapter 10.** As Melchizedek ministers bread and wine (the body and blood of the Lord Jesus) to Abraham after the slaughter of the kings, so the sacrifice and the blood of Jesus is ministered to our consciences to purge dead works. This allows us to serve the living God! Additionally, in these chapters (**Hebrews 9 and Hebrews 10**) we also learn that the better blood of Jesus "matures" our consciences through the purification in the shed blood of Jesus.

Romans 15:15-16 Introduction

In **Romans chapter 15,** the great apostles Paul gave insight as to the work of the matured priesthood relative to the New Covenant ministering to the Gentile nations. In Paul's writing we will see the work of the Melchizedek order as it relates to preaching the gospel of the Lord Jesus and the sanctifying work of the Holy Spirit.

Revelation 1:1-22:21 Introduction

Finally, I will also cite several verses in the book of the Revelation of Jesus Christ that shows the work of Jesus' Melchizedek priesthood administering the goodness and the severity of God. This priesthood will eventually rule the "habitable world to come" with Jesus the Christ. Yes, the book of the Revelation of Jesus Christ reveals Christ, the High Priest and his Body of priesthood ministering the justice of God, both God's goodness and severity and eventual rulership over the entire kingdom under heaven.

Thus, I pray the Spirit of Wisdom and Revelation in the knowledge of Jesus according to the order of Melchizedek empower you. This empowerment will help you to "hear" the difficult teaching concerning the order of Melchizedek. May the mystery and the hidden wisdom of the Lord Jesus' Melchizedek's order be revealed to you. May the Lord Jesus according to the order of Melchizedek mature your conscience. May the eternal Spirit strengthen your inner man to be rooted and ground in the love of Christ. May you continue to hope until the end! May you hear and understand that all believer in Christ is part of Jesus' Melchizedek order of matured priesthood.

JESUS, THE MELCHIZEDEK HIGH PRIEST

Interpretation-The High Priest of God

In this section we will review the Lord Jesus being understood as the High Priest of God in things pertaining to God. We will do this by looking at some of the definitions of words as well as translation from the Greek words. We will also cross-references with other scriptures to provide clearer understanding of Jesus' High Priesthood relative to Melchizedek. That is, according to the writings in the book of Hebrews and the writings of apostles like Paul, Peter and John, all of the "patterns" in the Old Testament related to the Tabernacle Moses built and/or the associated Aaronic priesthood were "types" of God's "Temple" or "Tabernacle." This includes both His heavenly Temple/Tabernacle and the Temple/tabernacle of the Corporate Body, His Church on earth. With the Lord Jesus being the High Priest over God's House according to the order of Melchizedek. "'Therefore,' holy brothers, partakers of the heavenly calling, consider **the Apostle and High Priest** of our profession, **Christ Jesus"** (Hebrews 3:1)

Hebrews 5:1-Jesus' High Priest Appointment
Because every **High Priest** taken **out of** men is **appointed over** men in things **'towards' to** God, that he may **offer** both **gifts and sacrifices over sins.**

1. Appointed is defined as to place down (permanently), i.e. (figuratively) to designate, constitute, convoy -- appoint, conduct, make, ordain, set. Thus, the Lord Jesus was born as a man and appointed by God to be High Priest for His people, those on earth and those in heaven **(Philippians 2:5-9).**

2. High Priest is a Greek compound, "archiereus," with "archo" meaning beginning, rule, first, chief and "hiereus" meaning priest, sacred, and temple. Hence the translation for "archo" as "high," as in highest rank, or first rank. In addition, based on the Greek definition for "priests" (hiereus) and its associated root and derivatives, all the priests of God are also "sacred;" they serve the "temple;" and they are "holy." Thus, our High Priest, the Lord Jesus Christ, is the Highest Priest; He is the Highest Sacred; and He is the Hight Holy One in the "Priest Temple" of God (the priests temple both in heaven and on earth)

3. The Hebrew word for priest is Kohen (KoHeN). Thus, based on Hebrew pictograph or Hebrew hieroglyphics, one of the definitions of "KoHen" can be understood as one who "reveals" the "yes," with "yes" representing God's responses (i.e., God's biblically based opinions). That is, "KoHen" is the Hebrew word "ken" (or KeN) which means "yes," or "it is so" with an "H" inserted in the middle of the word KeN, with "H" carrying the meaning of to reveal, to behold, hey, look, etc.. Again, as said above, God's High Priest or God's royal priesthood in general are called to give God's biblically based opinions, and/or God's answers through the Holy Spirit speaking, prophesies, tongues with interpretation of tongues, etc.

4. High Priests are appointed in things pertaining to God, or as it reads in the Greek text things **"towards"** God. Some of the things towards God that High Priests perform are to make propitiations for the sins of the people (**Heb 2:17, Luke 18:13).** "Propitiation" is translated from a Greek word "hilaskomai." Hilaskomai, its associated root and derivatives, means cheerful

mercy, cheerful grace, atonement related to sins, and so on (**Luke 18:13, see Strong's #2433, #2434, #2436**). Therefore, God "cheerfully" atones us through His "mercy," transmitted to us from His High Priest, the Lord Jesus, through communion of the Holy Spirit and through His delegated royal priesthood. Thus, it is God's High Priest, the Lord Jesus who decides our eternal punishment or our eternal life based on sins unatoned (no repentance or forgiveness) or due to sins being atoned (forgiven through Jesus' blood). However, it must be understood that the heavenly Father has atoned (forgiven) our sins through the Lord Jesus Christ! All believers must appropriate this forgiveness through faith in the blood of Jesus Christ! There is only one caveat, He also requires that we forgive others as He forgives us (**Matt 6:12 w/Matt 6:14**).

5. High Priests also **offer** both gifts (plural) and sacrifices (plural). The offerings of Jesus, our High Priest, are prayers and supplications to God (**Heb 5:7**). It follows that, like Jesus, our Melchizedek High Priest, we, His royal priesthood according to the order of Melchizedek must also "be governed to prayer" (**Col 3:2, Mark 9:29, etc.**).

6. The High Priest offering also consist of the Lord Jesus who sacrificed Himself on our behalf (**Heb 9:26, Heb 7:27, Eph 5:2**). That is the High Priests offer both **gifts (plural)** and **sacrifices (plural)** to God on behalf of the people for sins. The Lord Jesus Christ is both the "gifts" and "sacrifices" of God (**Heb 9:23**). Here are examples of how the process works. God provides the **gifts** to the people. Jesus is the gift of God's love offered for us unto eternal life (**John 3:16**). The Holy Spirit is the gift of God's living water **to us (John 4:10 w/John 7:38-39)**.

There is the gift of grace that God give us through the Lord Jesus and His Holy Spirit (**Eph 2:8**). There are gifts of the Spirit (**Acts 10:45**). There is the gift of eternal life, and so on (**Rom 6:23**).

7. Other processes of the offering of gifts are that God the Holy Father, receives the **gifts** from His people. The heavenly Father receives the gift of giving glory to God, where glory means good opinion, good impression of being, etc. (**Rev 14:7**). We are to also offer the gift of giving God honor (**Rev 19:7**). Honor means money, price paid, value, and so on. Thus, we are to value God more than money!

8. God, the "Righteous Father" also provides the **sacrifices** of the Lord Jesus Christ to the people for their benefits (**Heb 9:23 w/Heb 9:19**). For example, the Lod Jesus. Jesus, our Melchizedek, offered the sacrifices of a broken spirit and a broken and crushed heart (**Ps 51:17, compare Matt 11:2**). Jesus was/is the sacrificial Ox (**Heb 9:23 w/Heb 9:19**). Jesus was/is the sacrificial Lord's goat (**Heb 9:23 w/Heb 9:19**). Jesus was/is the sacrificial Lamb of God (**Rev 5:6-10**). The Lord Jesus' body issued the sacrificial water and blood (**Heb 9:23 w/Heb 9:19**). In addition, the Lord Jesus eventually drank the sacrificial bitter vinegar on the cross (**Heb 9:23 w/Heb 9:19 w/John 19:30**).

9. In turn, Jesus our High Priest receives the **sacrifices** from the people. **There are spiritual sacrifices** we are to offer to the "Great-togetherness" (the oneness of the Heavenly Father, the Lord Jesus, and the Holy Spirit (**1 Peter 2:5**). There are the sacrifices of a broken spirit and a broken and crushed heart (**Ps 51:17, compare Matt 11:29**). There is the spiritual sacrifice of giving and receiving from one's apostle and other ministers (**Phil**

4:15-19). There is the sacrifice of faith (**Phil 2:17**). We are to present our bodies as living sacrifice **(Rom 12:1)**. There are the sacrifices of good-doing and fellowshipping (**Heb 13:16)**. There is the evening sacrifice of lifting hands to God (**Psalm 141:2)**. There are the sacrifices of praise, which is the fruit of our lips confessing His name (**Heb 13:15)**.

10. Also, the Lord Jesus offered sacrifices over (on behalf of) sins. That is, through Jesus' sacrifice all sins can be forgiven except for blasphemy against the Holy Spirit **(Mk 3:28-30)**. There is sin unto Death (the Second Death) and there are sins not unto death **(1 John 5:16)**. **Here are examples of sin unto death that is to be avoided at all costs.**

    a. The sin unto Death of blasphemy against the Holy Spirit is to be avoided **(Mark 3:28-30)**.

    b. The sin unto Death of crucifying Jesus again is to be spurned **(Heb 6:4-8, Rev 11:8)**.

    c. The sin unto Death of blaspheming God's Name and His Tabernacle is to be rejected even if it means death in this life **(Rev 13:6 w/Rev 19:20 w/Rev 20:14)**.

11. That is, all sins can be forgiven except for spiritually crucifying[2] Jesus again **(Heb 6:4-8 w/Rev 11:8)**. All sins can be forgiven except for willfully sinning **(Heb 10:26-30)**. "Willfully" is translated from a Greek word "hekousiós," which means to act voluntarily, to consent, unforced, and intentional action. The Greek root for "willfully" is "hek." Which emphasizes intentional, deliberate action (choice). Please reference **1 Peter 5:2** where "willfully" is opposite to being "forced" or

---

[2] See notes in this volume on Hebrews 6:1-8

"constrained" to do something. Finally, all sins can be forgiven unless you cannot forgive-**Mat 6:12-15**

Hebrews 5:2-Jesus Measures Sufferings
Being-powerful to-measure-sufferings to-the ignorant, and on them that are **seduced**; for that he himself also is **around-laid** with **weakness**.

1. Priests are able to **measure-sufferings, which means they are literally able to "measure-emotions"** of their human peers. This is understood by the Greek definition for the word translated as "compassion" in the King James Version. "Compassion" is from a compound of the base of metrios (in due measure) and pathos (suffering, emotions). The Lord Jesus was able to **measure** the length of time of the weakness of the man at the pool **(John 5:1-8).** The Lord Jesus, our High Priest and His Melchizedek priesthood can measure the emotional suffering of the people, because Jesus and His priests themselves can identify with human weaknesses **(Heb 2:17-18).**

2. Priests of God are able to measure emotions of the **ignorant sins. Pursuant to the Greek definitions of "ignorant," these "sins of the ignorant" can be classified as** "unknown" sins, or sins that are "ignored." Priests of God are also able to measure emotions of **sins related to seduction** (wandering). Thus, as previously stated, the Lord Jesus, our High Priest according to the order of Melchizedek, is able to measure the emotions of sins because he was tempted at all points like us **(Heb 4:15-16).**

3. **Note:** there is no mention of measuring the emotions of the ignorance or seduction of "idiotes" (idiots).

"Idiots" are those who only follow their own private opinions and are rude (**compare 2 Cor 11:6**). Idiots are those who are rude in speech (**see 2 Cor 11:6**). Idiots are those who interpret ("unloose" or "unpack") scriptures incorrectly due to not listening to the Lord Jesus and they do not speak from the Holy Spirit (**2 Pet 1:20, Mark 4:34**).

4. Idiots are also defined as those who are untrained, unpolished, unskilled, rude in words. However, even though the writer did not mention "idiots" as those the Priests of God measure their suffering, a person being with the Lord Jesus for years also heals "idiotes" ignorance (**Acts 4:13**). With all of the above understood, **there is also n**o mention of measuring-emotions of willful sins in **Heb 5:2 (Rom 6:15, Heb 10:26-30)**. It follows that all saints have a responsibility to live accountable to our Lord Jesus Christ!

Hebrews 5:3-Offering for Sins

And **through this** he **owes**, as **about** the people, so also **about** himself, to offer for sins.

1. Due to the God's priests' empowerment to measure the emotions of the priests' own weakness and other, the priests **owe** it to give offering to God for his own sins and the people's sins. These offerings include but not limited to praying to God on the priests' own behalf and on the people's behalf for the forgiveness of sins to be granted by the heavenly Father.

2. **Note:** Even though the High Priest or priests experience the emotions of the people and his own emotion, he/she must still hear God on behalf of the people through it all (**Heb 5:8**).

Hebrews 5:4-The Value of the Priesthood

And no man **is-taking** this **value to-himself,** but he that is called **'under'** God, as was Aaron.

1. As God chose Aaron in the Old Testament to be high priest, similarly, God "called" the Lord Jesus to the honor of the Melchizedek High priesthood. According to the scriptures, being called into God's priesthood is honorable and valued (money paid). It is worthy or honorable to note at this juncture that in **Titus 2:3,** women are included in the priesthood.

2. In **Titus 2:3, "presbutis" (Elder** women) are called "towering-priests," or "fitting-priests," for so the phrase **"becoming holiness"** is literally translated from the Greek word "hieroprepéss" ("hieron," sacred place, temple, priest) **and** "prépō" (fitting, to tower up).**That is, in Christ, it is also fitting for women to be part of the royal priesthood!** (See the section titled "Melchizedek Order Priest-Workers").

3. In this section, we also learn that priests are **"under"** God. That is, they are not in authority; however, they are "under" God's authority. No one (man, angels or any other of God's creation) is "in authority." God alone is "in authority!" Everyone and everything are **"under"** God's authority (**Matt 8:9 w/Rom 13:1). Everyone is to obey God's imperative as He is the absolute Righteous Father in His authority!**

Hebrews 5:5-Priesthood and Sonship

So also, Christ glorified not himself to be made **High Priest**; but he that said **to-him**, you are **my Son,** today have I **birthed** you.

1. Pursuant to Hebrews 5:5 (above), Hight Priesthood is defined or synonymous with Sonship. "Christ glorified not himself to be made **High Priest**; but he that said **to-him**, you are **my Son.**" Thus, it can be understood that Jesus' Melchizedek priesthood consists of the Lord Jesus, the Son, and His many brothers of the same wombs, also called sons. **(Gal 3:26, Gal 4:6-7, Rom 8:14-17, Rom 8:29, Eph 1).**

2. The Lord Jesus is High-Priests being born Son of God **(Luke 1:30)**. This is in contrast to the Aaronic priesthood which was by fleshly **"birth."** The Lord Jesus' Melchizedek priesthood is by Holy Spirit "birth" (**Matt 1:18-20)**. In similarity, the Lord Jesus' Royal Priesthood (His saints) is of a holy gene (**1 Pet 2:9)**. That is, the Lord Jesus is the beginning of the "gene" of God **(see Greek for "only begotten" in 1 John 4:9)**. Thus, a person must be born from above by the Holy Spirit to be a part of the Melchizedek order **(John 3:1-8)**. Saying another way, a person must believe that Jesus is the Christ to be born of God (**1 John 5:1)**. In addition, all of God's mature sons also function as God's "royal priesthood" (lit., kingly-priests), those birthed and matured through the Spirit of Christ (**1 Pet 2:9, Rev 5:10, Rev 20:6).**

Hebrews 5:6-Jesus Eternal High Priesthood
As he says also in **'another-different,**' you are **Priest, into the age, according to** the **order of Melchizedek.**

1. Jesus is the eternal High Priest "according to" the order of Melchizedek. "According to" is translated from the Greek word "kata," which means to come down from higher to a lower." Thus, the Lord Jesus' Priesthood functions **both** on earth ("down" from heaven) and

eternally ("into the age") (the Holy of Holies in the heavens). The words "for" and "ever" which is used often in the scriptures is better translated "into the age." What age?

2. There are several understandings of the phrase "into the age." That is, there are various vantage points of the eternal age in the invisible which our Lord functions in His omnipresence! The Lord Jesus lives into the age (the eternal age) (**Heb 7:15-21**). Jesus lives into the age, the Holy of Holies (**Heb 6:18-20**). Jesus was carried-through into the Second, behind the second veil in the heavenly tabernacle **(Heb 6:18-20 w/Heb 9:24-28)**. Jesus lives into the age, the heavens (**Heb 8:1**). Jesus lives into the age (the millennium age). The millennium age is the age of the resurrected king-priests saints. This is understanding is based on the dimensions (10 cubits x 10 cubits x 10 cubits = 1000 C^3) of the Holy of Holies in the "Tabernace of Set Time"**³** Moses built according to the heavenly pattern (**Ex 26:14-30**).

3. The Lord Jesus' "brothers of the same womb," the heavenly Father's other mature sons, also function as "priest-togetherness" "according to the **order** of Melchizedek" (**Gal 4:6 w/Rom 8:29 w/Heb 7:11; 7:12; 7:249, 1 Peter 2:9, Rev 20:6**). "Order" is translated from the Greek word "taxis," which means to arrange (military term), "an ordered troop" arranged in descending ranks.

---

³ You may refer to a few of my books *The Completion of the Ages, the Gate, the Door, the Veil, Ezekiel the House-the City-the Land Interpreting the Patterns* and *The Prophetic Patterns of the Two Witnesses*, etcetera for further discussion about the ages starting from the Law of Moses to the Millennium

a. Thus, there is the "order" of Melchizedek priesthood functioning in their "portion" of offering "incense" (prayer) (**Luke 1:8-9, Heb 5:6-7, Ps 141:2, Rev 5:8, Rev 8:3-5)**

b. The Melchizedek priestly "order" of functioning in the gifts of the Holy Spirit, especially relative to speaking in tongues, prophecy, interpretation of tongues, etc. (**1 Cor 14:40 w/1 Cor 14).**

c. Melchizedek priesthood "order" relates to steadfastness of faith-**Col 2:5**. Therefore, in the Melchizedek order, we walk by faith and not by sight, etc. (**2 Cor 5:7, Heb 11:5-6).**

4. The phrase "according to" is Greek word "kata" which can be defined as coming down from (i.e., from a higher to a lower plane with special reference to terminus (end point) (J. Thayer). "Kata" is also translated as "according to," about, after, against. The Melchizedek ministry comes "down" from a "higher" place (the Highest God) to bring things pertaining to God in the lower plane **into us** on earth.

5. Some understandings of the "order of Melchizedek" are as follows where the phrase "order of Melchizedek"[4] **is** used six (6) or seven (7) times in scriptures depending on which Greek text is used. The scriptural references for the use of the phrase "order of Melchizedek" are **Psalms 110:4, Hebrews 5:6, Hebrews 5:10, Hebrews 6:20, Hebrews 7:11, Hebrews 7:17, and Hebrews 7:21.**

a. Jesus used **Psalm 110** concerning the order of Melchizedek in reference to His enemies being made His footstool (**Matt 22:41-46).**

---

[4] Please refer to my book titled *Melchizedek* for further development of the order of Melchizedek related to God's seven oaths.

b. The context of all of **Hebrews 5:6** is that of the "calling" of Jesus as God's High Priest is according to the order of Melchizedek.

c. **Hebrews 5:9-10** is a reference to the Melchizedek order of Jesus being called to public places, not just having Church in a building. **"Called"** is a Greek compound word [prosagoreuo, "towards (pros)" and "marketplace (agora)," which can be translated as "towards-public square," etc.].

d. **Hebrews 6:20** references the order of Jesus according to the Melchizedek order as our **forerunner** into the Holy of Holies, where we also have a refuge[5] for an anchor for souls.

e. **Hebrews 7:11** references the order of Jesus who is now the Lawgiver that leads us to maturity, according to the order of Melchizedek.

f. The sixth mention of Jesus order according to Melchizedek relates to Jesus being the High "priest forever." The Greek text reads as such: "You are a priest **'into the age'** 'according-to' the order of Melchizedek."-**Heb 7:17.**

    i. In addition to the above references on the order of Melchizedek, it is honorable to the Lord Jesus to note that in **Hebrews 7:21** the heavenly Father has no regret with respect to the Son, the Lord Jesus. The phrase "will not repent," mean, "will not regret." God, the heavenly Father, has "no regrets" with regards to His Son Jesus, the Christ, being the High Priest forever (into the age) according to the

---

[5] The "Cities of Refuge" principle instituted by God through Moses and Joshua **(Joshua 20)**

order[6] of Melchizedek. The Lord Jesus is the Son, in whom the heavenly father is well pleases **(Mark 9. Matt 17, Luke 9).**

Hebrews 5:7-Jesus' Prayers as High-Priest

Who in the days of his flesh, when he had **offered** up **prayers** and **olive-branch-supplications** with **forceful screaming** and tears **towards** him that was **powerful** to save him **out of** death and was heard in that he **well-take**.

The offerings of the Lord Jesus, according to the order of Melchizedek, also include prayers and supplications. Yes, offerings of prayers and supplication were part of Jesus' offering for sins. The Lord Jesus' offerings of "prayers" **were "towards" <u>God</u>** for the "needs" of the people. The Lord did not pray toward persons or people. This is a function of the Melchizedek priesthood. When we pray, we pray to God and not towards people. With that said, here are the perspectives of the offerings of prayers and supplication of our Lord Jesus to God. Prayers are also defined as to be in want, or heart-felt need.

1. Prayer. In Hebrews 5:7, is defined entreaty due to indigence (lacking comfort of life). Prayer is also defined as to bind, to begging for self-need.
2. Supplication means extending an olive branch seeking peace. It follows that our Lord prayed and supplicated forcefully to God as our High Priest.

---

[6] **Note**: The Majority Texts (Byzantine Texts) and the later received text are the text which uses the word "order" in Hebrews 7:21. The word "order" is not found in the Alexandrian Texts (arguable considered to be the oldest text).

3. Our Lord Jesus prayed with "loud outcries" (Greek: krazon (transliterated as "crazy"). Yes, the Lord's prayer sounded crazy sometimes as he interceded to God.

4. Our Lord shed tears in prayer often. He did this in the **days (plural)** of His flesh.

5. Jesus' prayer was "towards" His heavenly Father. The Lord Jesus understood that only the heavenly Father could help Him out of death. He knew only God could deliver Him out of the death of indigence, the lack of comfort of life (linked to death), hardship due to poverty (linked to death), and deprivation (link to death).

6. The heavenly Father **"heard"** the Lord Jesus' prayers and supplications. This is also an important truth, and the question must be asked: why did the heavenly Father hear the Lord Jesus? The heavenly Father heard the Lord Jesus because He "took" His emotional situation "well." That is, the word "feared" in the reference above is the Greek compound word "eulabés" (eu (well) + labes (take). It means to take a situation well through reverence or respect for the living God. Noah did the same thing. Noah **"well-take"** God's decision when God **warned** him of the flood to come that would destroy the world (the unrighteous heaven and the unrighteous earth) that was then (**Heb 11:7, 2 Peter 3**).

7. **Note:** The English word translated "warn" used to document God's warning to Noah of the impending flood can be understood as follows: "Warn" is found under **Strong's #5537, and #5536.** "Warn" is the Greek word "cherma," which mean to utter an oracle (compare the original sense; i.e., divinely intimate; compare the secular sense, to constitute a firm for

business, i.e. (generally) bear as a title, to be called, be admonished (warned) of God, reveal, speak. "Cherma" means to transact business, especially to manage public affairs; to advise or consult with one about public affair; to make answer to those who ask advice, present inquiries, or requests, etc.; used of judges, magistrates, rulers, kings.

    i. Thus, as God and Noah used their own business and money to make the Ark. Therefore, like apostle Paul, ministers of the gospel should also use their businesses (if they have one), or use their occupations to fund the work of God; and they should not solely depend on or abuse the saint in giving **(Acts 20:33-35, Acts 18:1-3)**. With that said, "cherma" also means to give a response to those consulting an oracle and money that is useful **(Strong's #5536).**

Hebrews 5:8-Emotions and Obedience

Though he was Son yet learned he **obedience (under-hearing) from** the things which he **emotion.**

1. The Lord Jesus learned obedience through "suffering" even though He was a mature Son and the Heir of God.
2. "Suffering" is translated from the Greek word "pascho," which is defined as feeling heavy **emotions or to** experience strong sensation. Thus, sonship in God does not exempt a person from suffering emotionally.
3. The Lord Jesus "obeyed" what he "heard under" the heavenly Father in spite of His emotional challenges. That is, the word "obey" is a Greek compound word meaning "to hear-under." Thus, emotional sufferings are also used to teach us to hear God.

Hebrews 5:9-Jesus, the Causer
And **'being-matured,'** he became the **'causer'** of **eternal** salvation **to** all them that **obey** (**under-hear**) him.

1. The Lord Jesus was **matured** through sufferings, both emotionally and physically (**Heb 2:10, Heb 5:8-9**).
2. He was mature emotionally in all three realms of His Sonship [mature spirit, mature soul and matured in the flesh dimension (He was dead to the lust of the flesh)].
3. The Lord Jesus was also matured related to eternal resurrection. With that said, below are some principles related to a matured character.
4. "Maturity" in the reference above, by definition, means to reach a goal or aim. Therefore, the Lord Jesus reached God's goal or aim as the first fully grown "Man" (**Eph 4:13, John 4:29**).
5. Pursuant to the writing of **Ephesians 4:13 and Mark 11:12-14,** it can be understood that a matured man has "the faith of God." The is a difference between having faith in God and having the faith of God. The Lord Jesus had the faith of God that creates instantaneous results (**Eph 4:13, Mk 11:22 w/Mk 11:12-14 w/MK 11:20-26**).
6. A matured person has the knowledge of God, ascertaining to the same knowledge of the Son of God (**Eph 4:13, Rev 19:12-13**).
7. Per **1 Cor 13:4-13,** a mature person characterizes the love of God. The Lord Jesus is God's love personified.
8. A mature man/woman does not cause "falls" with his/her words (**James 3:2**).
9. A matured man/woman of love demonstrates the delivery of exact prophecies (predictions), word of wisdom (clear words to complete a task skillfully), or word of knowledge (present knowing of a situation in a

person's life. The Lord Jesus established this attribute skillfully. (**John 4:14-30, I Cor 3:4-13).**

10. We are to be matured in conscience, through cleansing by the blood of Jesus, through faith in His blood (**Heb 9:14 w/Heb 10:1-4, Rom 3:25)**

11. Maturity is also defined as eternal life "into the age" by resurrection (**Heb 7:28).** Thus, part of a believer's mature state is the blessing of the resurrection unto eternal life, with an understanding that resurrection or glorified bodies are related to enduring suffering in this life. The Lord experienced intense emotions through the pains of death **(Acts 2:24).** And He was resurrected (matured) to His eternal state, the eternal state of life "into the age."

12. Maturity also relates to spirit maturity. In fact, in heaven, there are spirits of Just men made matured (**Heb 12:23).** If follows that a person's spirit can be dwarfed through bondages and anger (see the books of Exodus and Ecclesiastes). The Apostle Paul taught that believers' maturity is to be spirit, soul, and body[7] **(1 Thess 5:23).**

13. In **Hebrews 5:9,** we also learn that the Lord Jesus also became the "Author" [literally, the Causer (by request for something due)] of eternal salvation. Thus, it is our Lord Jesus who requested of God on our behalf to also inherit eternal salvation. Yes, it is the Lord Jesus, our High-Priest, who asked God to grant us eternal life. One caveat though, as Jesus obeyed (hear-under) His heavenly Father, we must also obey (under-hear) Jesus' Melchizedek's Priesthood **(Heb 5:8-9)!**

---

[7] You may refer to my book *Wholly Maturing and Wholly Inheriting Spirit, Soul and Body* for additional development

MELCHIZEDEK, DIFFICULT TO INTERPRET

Interpretation-The Unveiling of Melchizedek

The understanding of Melchizedek and his order as they relate to the Lord Jesus and His Body of royal priests are very difficult to understand and difficult to translate or interpret. That is, Melchizedek and his order are only mentioned twice in the Old Testament. Melchizedek is also referenced (hinted) by our Lord Jesus Christ relative to Psalm 110 and King David. Jesus, our Melchizedek, and Jesus' order is also taught in the brook of Hebrews. Thus, God's deliberate veiling of Melchizedek and his order, as they relate to the Lord Jesus, is not easy to understand (unveil) without a willingness to **hear** about this more excellent ministry of the High Priesthood of Jesus, the Christ.

Hebrews 5:10-Jesus "Called" Melchizedek

Called (lit., 'towards-market-place') 'under' God a High Priest,' according to **the order of Melchizedek.**

1. The word "called" used in Hebrews 5:10 means to address in an assembly. It is not the Greek word "kleo" typically used translated to the English word "call."
2. The Greek word and its derivative used for "call" in Hebrews 5:10 literally means "to harangue (lengthy aggressive speech), "towards the market place," towards the public assembly, and so on.
3. That is, the Greek word translated as "call" is "prosagoreuó" [pro (towards) and agoreuo (harangue in the market place)]. Thus, the Lord Jesus' ministry was also towards those in the market place sometimes with aggressive speech towards them **(Luke 16:1-18)**.

4. The phrase **"by God"** reads as **"under the God"** in the Greek text. Melchizedek ministry is "called," under the authority of God, to minister in both the public places and the assemblies of God (**John 18:20**). **As previously** indicated under **Hebrews 5:4** notes, only God is "in" authority, all else is "under" His authority.

5. The phrase "order of Melchizedek" is used six (6) or seven (7) times in scriptures depending on which Greek text is used in addition to the Old Testament. As previously indicated under the notes for **Hebrews 5:6**, the scriptural references for the use of the phrase "order of Melchizedek" are **Psalms 110:4, Hebrews 5:6, Hebrews 5:10, Hebrews 6:20, Hebrews 7:11, Hebrews 7:17, and Hebrews 7:21.**

   a. Jesus used **Psalm 110** concerning the order of Melchizedek in reference to His enemies being made His footstool **(Matt 22:41-46).**

   b. The context of all of **Hebrews 5:6** is that of the "calling" of Jesus as God's High Priest is according to the order of Melchizedek.

   c. **Hebrews 5:9-10** is a reference to the Melchizedek order of Jesus being called to public places, not just having Church in a building.

   d. **Hebrews 6:20** references the order of Jesus according to the Melchizedek order as our forerunner into the Holy of Holies, where also we have a refuge for an anchor for souls.

   e. **Hebrews 7:11** references the order of Jesus who is now the Lawgiver that leads us to maturity, according to the order of Melchizedek.

   f. The sixth mention of Jesus order according to Melchizedek relates to Jesus being the High "priest forever."

Hebrews 5:11-Melchizedek Difficult to Explain

About whom we have many things to say, and **'difficult (to) translate**,' seeing you are **'lazy'** of hearing.

1. The phrase "hard to be uttered" used in the King James Version is a compound word from the Greek suffix "dus" and "herméneuó."
   a. Duserméneutos, pronounced as doo-ser-MAY-noo-tos literally means "difficult to be translated," or "difficult to be interpreted," or "difficult to explain."
2. Therefore, understanding the truth of the mystery of Melchizedek is difficult. However, God provided a way to understand the mystery of Jesus' Melchizedek order. The Holy Spirit, through the writer of the book of Hebrews, taught that the mystery of the Melchizedek order can be **"explained"** through **"translation"** and contextual **"interpretation."**
3. Melchizedek's principles are understood foremost by **"translation:"**
   a. We can understand the mystery of Melchizedek by the translation of Melchizedek's name.
   b. We can understand the mystery of Melchizedek by the translation of the words associated with Melchizedek.
   c. We can understand the mystery of Melchizedek by the translation of the City associated with Melchizedek.
   d. We can understand the mystery of Melchizedek by interpreting what is <u>unsaid</u> about Melchizedek (i.e., there no mention of him being fathered, mothered, or having genealogy)

4. **Note:** The hidden truth related to Melchizedek are part of the hidden mysteries of God that God reveals to those who love Him **(1 Cor 2:9-10).**
    a. This mystery of Jesus's High Priesthood being according to the order of Melchizedek was hidden from Moses, angels, generations, ages, etc. (**Heb 7:11-15, Eph 3:5; 3:9)**
    b. The understanding of the Lord Jesus High Priesthood being according to the order of Melchizedek is only revealed by the Holy Spirit (**Heb 9:8, 1 Cor 2:9-19, Eph 3:5)**
    c. Thus, the workings of the Melchizedek order are part of the "hidden wisdom" of God revealed by the Holy Spirit to the "mature" in Christ (**Heb 9:8, 1 Cor 2:9-10)**
5. The phrase "dull of hearing" used of immature saints also mean "lazy of hearing," or sluggish of hearing, or slow to hear, or inert of hearing.
    a. A person who is dull of hearing is not prepared to hear the meat of the teaching related to King Jesus, our Melchizedek, and His order of royal priesthood.

Hebrews 5:12-Teachers versus Milk Drinkers

Because when **through** the **time** you **'owe'** to be teachers, you **have need** that one teaches you again **what-is** the **'elements' of-the 'original' of-the** oracles of God; and are become such as have need of milk, and not of **'stiff food.'**

1. The word translated as time is the Greek word "chronos," and it means uninterrupted time.
2. The believers "owed" it to be teachers by now due to the time they have been taught by others. However, they needed to be taught again. Thus, it is understood

from the context of Hebrews 5:12, God's teachers have the ability to hear things difficult to interpret.

    a. However, the Hebrews saints needed to be taught **again** the following:

        i. The Hebrew saints needed to be taught again elementary things. They had to relearn "things in a row, things in rank, and things series." They could not be taught the unheard mystery of Melchizedek relative to the Lord Jesus, or the illogical meats of God's Word related to Melchizedek.

        ii. The Hebrew saints had to be retaught by walking them through lines of teachings (precept upon precept) **(Isa 28:10)**.

        iii. They also had to be retaught the beginning of the Word of God **(Heb 6:1-2)**.

3. The beginning of the Word of God or the Word of Christ is called "milk."

    a. Milk is for saints who can only understand logical teachings (In **1 Peter 2:2,** "word" is literally transliterated as "logical").

    b. Milk is for saints who are untried in the Word of righteous-togetherness **(Heb 5:13)**

        i. We are only righteous because we are "together" with the Lord Jesus through faith in Him, faith in His blood and the baptism of the Holy Spirit.

        ii. In Christ, this "togetherness" with the Lord Jesus will be tested.

4. Stiff food is food for the "mature." Since milk also means logical words (teachings), "meat" is illogical words (teachings).

    a. The teaching concerning Melchizedek is not always logical to the unspiritual senses.

b. Therefore, only those who have their senses trained to discern both good and evil can understand the mystery of the Melchizedek order.

Hebrews 5:13-Untested in Righteousness

For everyone that **'partner' of-milk** is **'un-probe-tested'** in the Word of **'righteous-togetherness:'** for he is **an 'infant.'**

1. Pursuant to the writing of **Hebrews 5:13** in conjunction with **1 Peter 2:2,** we see that milk is for saints who can only understand logical teachings **(1 Peter 2:2)**
2. Pursuant to the reading of **Hebrews 5:13,** we see that milk is for saint's who are untried in the Word of righteousness, **the Word of right-togetherness (Heb 5:13).**
3. The word "babe" is also defined as an infant. Thus, "babes in Christ" are immature believers. Below are some of the biblical definitions of a babe or an infant.
    a. Baby saints are zealots (hot, boiling) in a negative way **(1 Cor 3:2-4, Gal 4:18).**
    b. Baby saints are quarrelsome **(1 Cor 3:2-4)**
    c. Babby saints are divisive **(1 Cor 3:2-4)**
    d. Baby saints can only understand logical teaching **(1 Pet 2:2)**
    e. Baby saints are untested in the Word of righteousness-togetherness **(Heb 5:13).** For example, these are testing that sees if you will hold on to Jesus' righteousness when emotions seem contrary.
    f. Baby saints are no different from slaves (not entrusted with absolute ownership rights given by God to govern our spiritual enemies, given to subdue the earth [not people, and so on **(Gal 4:1)**].

g. Baby saints are under guardians and house-lawyers **(Gal 4:2)**.

Hebrews 5:14-Matured Discernment

But **'stiff food' 'to-them'** that are **'mature,'** even those who **'through habit'** have their senses **'naked-exercised'** to **'through-judge'** both **'ideal'** and evil.

1. The stiff food of God's words represents meat or food for the "mature."
    a. The meat of God's words represents teaching that appears to be illogical.
2. The meat of God words is to be given to those who by reason of "use" or "habit" have their senses trained to consume meat.
3. The word exercise is literally transliterated as "gymnasium," which means to train naked.
    a. Thus, all saints should be transparent before the Lord having nothing hidden **(Proverbs 15:11)**. God already knows all things, so it behooves us to be honest (naked)before Him **(Gen 2:25, Heb 4:12-13)**.
4. Saints, through proper teaching and "use" of what is taught is to develop their senses to discern. Discern is the Greek word "diakrisis," which means to thoroughly judge, to distinguish, etcetera.
5. Those who have their **senses** trained to discern between good and evil can understand the Melchizedek Order.
    a. We are to develop our hearing. **Job 12:11** gives an excellent simile of how to discern by hearing.
    b. We are to develop our sense of spiritual smelling (**1 Cor 12:17**).

   c. We can taste the things of God and sometimes the things that are not of God. The Lord's grace taste good! (**Heb 6:5, 1 Peter 2:1-3).**

   d. The Lord Jesus also demonstrated a tremendous sensing through touching (**Mark 6:30).**

   e. Our spirits can also develop the sense of exact knowing ["epiginous" (upon-knowing, exact-knowing)] (**Mark 2:8).**

   f. Seeing by the Lord Jesus, through the Holy Spirit is also a powerful tool of discernment (**Rev 2:18-23, Luke 11:17, Luke 9:47, Matt 9:4).**

6. When we develop all six senses (yes six senses), we will be able to discern both **good (attractive, ideal)** and **bad (intrinsic)**

   a. Thus, with developed senses, the teaching about Melchizedek should be "attractive" to the mature

   b. To the underdeveloped senses, the teaching about Melchizedek seems "bad."

   c. However, the mystery of the Melchizedek ministry can be **heard, seen, tasted, touched, smelled,** and **known** by the revelation of the Holy Spirit for the matured (**1 Cor 2:6-7).**

MELCHIZEDEK, JESUS, THE MATURE ONE

Interpretation-The Stages of Maturing

One of the many things the Spirit of the Lord opened to me concerning Melchizedek is his "greatness" as we will exegete in **Hebrews 7:4** in a later section. "Greatness," used in **Hebrews 7:4,** by definition means, distinguished excellence, adult, full grown, mature, and so on. Thus, maturity is one of the "goals" of Jesus' Melchizedek order. Melchizedek foreshadowed the maturity and adulthood, our Lord Jesus demonstrated to the fullest. That is, our Lord Jesus's teachings and actions are the very image of the Melchizedek order that the royal priesthood of God is to attain unto in maturity. This is accomplished as the Spirit of the Lord Jesus increases us (grows us up) through the stages of maturity (which can be simplified into three (3) stages: child, young man, and fatherhood).

Hebrews 6:1-3-Going to the Mature One

[1]**Through-which** leaving the **beginning** of the **Word** of Christ, **let-us-be-carried upon the Mature-One**; not **laying** again the **foundation** of **repentance** from dead works, and of faith **upon** God, [2]of the **teaching** of baptisms, **both** of laying on of hands, and of resurrection **both** of the dead, and of **eternal judgment-result**. [3]And this will we do, if God permit.

1. To understand the Melchizedek order, we must move on from beginning things of the Word of Christ (foundational teachings) unto the Mature-one (Christ, Jesus). There are levels of "growing up" ("maturing") growing from "the beginning of the Word of Christ" to becoming an adult priest according to the order of Melchizedek (**1 John 5:1 w/1 John 2:13-14).**

a. The first of the four principles of maturing is a person **must be born again (1 John 5:1, John 3:1-21)**

   i. A baby in Christ is considered "untaught" in the Word of God **(Gal 4:1, 1 Pet 2:1, 1 Cor 3:1)**

   ii. A baby in Christ is considered as "non-speaking" **(Strong's #3516, 1 Cor 13:11). That is,** babes in Christ do not know how to use the "spoken" Word of God against Satan (one can **contrasts the "mature" Jesus use of the spoken word in Mat 4:1-11).**

   iii. Babes in Christ are saints who are zealots (hot, boiling). They boil over in attitudes **(1 Cor 3:2-4)**

     a. Note: Zeal can used for good or bad **(Gal 4:17-18, etc.).**

   iv. Babes in Christ are saints who have a propensity to quarrel **(1 Cor 3:2-4).**

   v. Babes in Christ are saints who are divisive **(1 Cor 3:2-**4)

   vi. Babes in Christ are saints who can only understand logical teaching **(1 Pet 2:2).** That is, babies in Christ have a challenging time grasping illogical (meaty) teaching (compare **John 3:9 w/John 3:1-9)**

   vii. Babes in Christ are saints who are un-tested in the Word of righteousness-togetherness **(Heb 5:13).** The heavenly Father will test believers as part of their maturing process **(Luke 4:1-13, 1 Pet 1:6-9). Note:** God does not test us with evil-**James 1:13**

   viii. Babes are saints who are no different from "slaves" (they are not entrusted with absolute ownership rights until they mature in Christ) **(Gal 4:1)**

   ix. Baby saints are those who are under guardians and house-lawyer **(Gal 4:2).** That is, as a natural baby, babes in Christ always has to "turn" to someone more mature to "guide" them.

b. **The second of the four principles of maturing is growing from a baby to a "child" (Greek word "paidia" used of a child in training, 1 John 2:13-14).**

   i. A child in the Lord Jesus is a saint who is being taught **the six-facets of the foundation** of Christ or the beginning principles of Christ (**Heb 6:1-2**)

      1. A saint who is "child" in the Spirit and Word of God must be taught repentance from dead works. This repentance from dead works enhances a saint's ability to serve the living God (**Heb 6:1-2, Heb 9:14**).

      2. A child in the Lord Jesus, is to be taught to have faith towards God. They are taught of God existence. All saints must believe that the living God exists (**Heb 11:5-6**). A saint is to be taught that the living God rewards those who "seek" things "out of" God (**Heb 6:1-2, Heb 11:5-6**).

      3. A spiritual child in the Lord is to be taught the doctrines (plural) of baptism (**Heb 6:1-2**)

         a. There is water baptism (**1 Peter 3:20-22**)

         b. There is Holy Spirit baptism (**Acts 11:16-17**)

         c. There is baptism of crucifixion (**Luke 12:50, Mk 10:39**)

         d. There is also baptism of fire (**Matt 3:11**)

      4. Laying on of hands is also a beginning principle for a spiritual child (**Heb 6:1-2**).

         a. A spiritual child must learn that through the laying of hands the Holy Spirit can be received (**Acts 19:6**).

    b. There is also the teaching related to laying hands on a sick person to impart healing (**Acts 28:8**)

    c. **Note:** Do not lay hands on anyone too quickly-**1 Tim 5:22**

5. A "child" in the Lord should also be taught about the resurrection of the dead as one of the six facets of the foundation of the beginning principles of Christ (**Heb 6:1-2**).

    a. The resurrection of the dead is in phases.

      i. Jesus' Resurrection was also in two phases. Jesus is the first fruit (preeminent phase), then some of the saints were also resurrected after Him (**Matt 27:50-53, 1 Cor 15:20**).

      ii. The first resurrection is also in two phases. There is the resurrection of the First fruit Christ (phase 1), then there is the second phase of those who are Christ's in Jesus' coming (**1 Cor 15:23 w/Rev 11**).

6. The sixth facet of the six-facets of the beginning principles of Christ the resurrection of eternal judgment (**Heb 6:1-2**).

    a. At the eternal judgment there will be the resurrection of the rest of the dead who were not raised in the first resurrection.

      i. Those found written in the book of life will be given eternal life (**Rev 20:12-15, John 5:28-29**).

      ii. At the eternal judgment, those not found written in the Book of life will be given eternal punishment (**Rev 20:12-15, Mat 25:46**)

c. **The third of the four principles of maturity is growing into a young man translated from the Greek word neanisko (1 John 2:13-14)**

   i. A spiritual young man/woman represents a saint who have become strong in Christ and through Christ Jesus **(1 John 3:14)**

   ii. A young man represents a saint who conquered the wicked one **(1 John 2:13)**

      1. Conquer is defined as to defeat an enemy.

   iii. A young man is a saint having been enlightened in Christ (**Heb 6:4-5**).

   iv. A young man in Christ is those who have developed taste related to tasting the heavenly gift (**Heb 6:4-5**). The heavenly gift can include the grace of our Lord Jesus **(Heb 6:4-5, 1 Peter 2:3)**.

   v. A young man in Christ is a saint developed into tasting "partnering" with the Holy Spirit (**Heb 6:4-5**). **The Holy Spirit sent down from heaven partners with** those preaching the gospel, and the preaching of the gospel can be tasted (**Heb 6:4-5,1 Pet 1:12**)

   vi. A young man in Christ developed tasting of the good rhema of God (**Heb 6:4-5**). This principle can represent a saint tasting the power (ability, results) of hearing God's living voice (**Luke 1:37-38, Rom 10:14-17**)

   vii. A young man is represented in a saint who can taste the powers of the impending age-**Heb 6:4-5. Yes, the power of the age to come can be tasted;** those experiencing God's great power related to resurrection and reigning with Christ (**Acts 4:33, Rev 11:17, Rev 20:1-6, Heb 2:1-10**).

d. **The fourth of the four stages of growth is maturing into a father (Greek: "patér"), which means a progenitor (begetter), an originator, a provider, a protector (1 John 2:13-14).**

    i. Per the beloved apostle John, "fathers know the Lord Jesus from the beginning" **(1 John 2:13-14).** This speaks of knowledge gained about the heavenly Father, the Lord Jesus, and the Holy Spirit through longevity with the Lord Jesus **(John 15:27)**

    ii. Fathers' are those who have been with Christ in longevity [(from their beginning as a babe in Christ unto their maturity becoming as Christ) bear witness of the Lord Jesus) **John 15:27]**. Thus, one of the facets of becoming a father is to have the "beginning" of the Word of Christ in practice and not just in information **(Heb 6:1, Heb 5:12)**

    iii. Per, the beloved apostle John, "fathers know Him (God, Christ) from the beginning" **(1 John 2:13-14)**. That is, one of the principles related to being identified as "fathers" is having knowledge from the Spirit of God related to knowledge **of** the beginning. This knowledge of the beginning can include, but not limited to the following:

        1. Mature knowledge of the beginning related to the Word and God **(John 1:1)**

        2. Mature knowledge of God's definition of marriage from the beginning **(Mark 10:6)**

        3. God's knowledge relative to Satan and Satan's sins, lies, murders from the beginning **(John 8:44, 1 John 3:8, Rev 12:9)**

        4. Understanding of Judas (betrayers) from the beginning **(John 6:64)**

    iv. Fathers in the Lord Jesus has mature knowledge of the "Beginning Priesthood" of Jesus our Melchizedek (**Heb 5:10, Heb 3:1, Heb 8:1, Heb 9, etc.)**

    v. Fathers in the Lord demonstrate the character nature of love (**1 John 3:1, 1 John 4:10, 1 John 4:8)**

    vi. Fathers "exhort" (call-beside), fathers bring "closure" to unsolved circumstance and fathers "witness" of the Lord Jesus "with evidence" (**1 Thess 2:11)**

    vii. Fathers procreate children through the gospel (**1 Cor 4:15, Phil 2:22)**

    viii. Fathers lay up for their children (spiritual and natural), being willing to be spent for their children (**2 Cor 12:14-15)**

2. With all that was said above concerning the six-facets of foundation related to the beginning principles of Christ, the Hebrews Christians, and all saints we are encouraged to move forward the Mature-one (Christ, Jesus).

    a. The Mature One whom we are to move towards in maturity is the Lord Jesus, our distinguished Melchizedek (**Heb 5:6-6:1, Heb 12:2 w/Heb 6:1).**

        i. Remember the context of **Hebrews 6** is in reference to believers maturing in their "senses" to learn about and put into practice the mature, distinguished order of our Melchizedek, the Lord Jesus Christ in this life and in the next millennium.

    b. Maturity is walking in the adulthood of Melchizedek exactly as the Lord Jesus imaged the heavenly Father (**Heb 5:6-6:1 w/Heb 7:4)**

        i. Melchizedek's "greatness" is defined as: distinguished, adult, full grown, etc. (this principle of maturity will be exegeted in the section on **Hebrews 7)**

c. Jesus is the Causer and Mature One of our faith-**Heb 12:2.** How was Jesus' maturity displayed in this context of being the Causer and Matured One of our faith? Because of "the joy set before him:"

  1. The Lord Jesu endured the crucifixion (**Heb 12:2**)

  2. He despised the shame of contradictions He experienced **(Heb 12:3)**

  3. The Lord Jesus resisted unto blood striving against sin (**Heb 12:4**)

Hebrews 6:4-5-Enlightened Ones

⁴Because, **impossible** for those who were once enlightened, having tasted **both** of the heavenly gift, and **became partners** of the **Holy Spirit**, ⁵And have tasted the **'attractive'** **'Declaration'** of God, the powers **both** of the **age** **'impending.'**

1. Hebrew 6:4-5, cited above, as it reads in the interlinear, lists the things that if a person is enlightened by them and decides to fall away from the Lord Jesus, they cannot be renewed into repentance again. These enlightenments are as follows:

a. Those who are enlightened by tasting the heavenly gift. This heavenly gift can represent the grace of our Lord Jesus that can be tasted (**1 Peter 2:3**)

b. Those who are enlightened by tasting partnering with the Holy Spirit. This can represent those preaching the gospel with Holy Spirit sent down from heaven (**1 Pet 1:12**)

c. Those who are enlightened by tasting of the good rhema of God. This can represent those tasting the power of hearing God's living voice (**Luke 1:37-38**)

d. Those who are enlightened by tasting the powers of the impending age. Those experiencing God's great power related to resurrection and reigning with Christ **(Acts 4:33, Rev 11:17, Rev 20:1-6, Heb 2:1-10)**

Hebrews 6:6-Wrongly Crucifying Jesus Again

If they shall **'beside-fall,'** to **'up-fresh'** them again **into repentance**; **'the-ones-again-crucifying to-themselves'** the Son of God, and **beside-exhibit-him**.

1. For those who tasted the enlightenments listed in the previous verses **(Hebrews 6:4-5),** it is impossible to renew those who **"fall-way"** from the Son of God after being enlightened.

2. Those who are "enlightened" are treated differently from those who are having foundation laid with beginning principles, **if they fall away**. A few examples of falling away are as follows:

   a. Falling away (or literally to fall beside) means to "fall" from "beside" God's "love" into "fear" by eating of the fruit of duality (good and evil). This fruit of duality can generate dueling internal speech rejecting the presence of God through self-consciousness because of one's nakedness before God **(Gen 3:8-11)**

   b. Falling away can also mean falling away from belief in God's love for you by seeing God and His voice as someone to be avoided **(Gen 3:8-11, w/1 John 4:8).**

   c. Falling away are also those who apostatize from God by not "welcoming **the love of the Truth** that they may be saved" **(2 Thes 2:10 w/2 Thes 2:3-4)**

   d. Those falling away are those who become un-pursuable through bitterness and expecting God to always "prove" Himself to them **(Heb 3:7-19)**

e. Those who fall away are those crucifying Jesus again. This crucifying Jesus again can represent those who participate in Mystery Babylon's acts of sodomy and practices of Egypt (**Rev 11:8, 2 Tim 3:8, Ex 7, Ex 8, 1 Cor 10:19-21, Ezek. 16:49, Gen 19, etc.**). The enlightened ones who fall away openly exhibit the Son of God as crucified again **(Heb 10:26-29)**. Therefore, the enlightened person cannot be renewed to repentance if they make public shame the Lord Jesus Christ.

f. **Note:** Baby Christians in the Lord Jesus can be renewed to repentance if they sin **(1 John 2:1-2, 1 John 1:9-10)**. Thus, **Hebrew 6:4-6** is referencing believers who fall away from Christ having moved on from foundation principles, being babes, to enlightenment.

Hebrews 6:7-Blessings for Cultivation

For the earth which drinks in the rain that come often upon it, and brings forth herbs **'well-placed'** for them **through** whom it is **'land-worked,' 'change-taking'** blessing from God:

1. God expect us to produce vegetation appropriate for Him who waters us.
   a. A person who plants a cabbage patch expects cabbage to grow (**1 Cor 3:5-9**).
   b. Thus, God expects fruits in our lives when we are watered with the Word of God
2. God, Himself, receives blessing when His "watered" people produces appropriate vegetation (fruit of the Spirit)
   a. A person who plants tomatoes seeds expects to receive the blessings of eating the tomatoes.

Hebrews 6:8-Thorns and Briers

Yet that which bears thorns and **briers** is **'not-seem-approved'** and is **near to 'down-curse;'** whose **finish** is **into** 'burning.'

1. Thorns and briers are defined as those who crucify the Son of God **again.**
2. Thorns and briers are those who are exhibiting the Son of God **crucified** a **second time** by turning back to the "pollutions of the world," turning back to animal sacrifices for sins, and so on (**2 Pet 2:20-22, Heb 10:26-27, Jude 1:3-5**)
3. The judgment for crucifying the Son of God again is to be **cursed.**
4. The judgment for crucifying the Son of God again is **burning.**
   a. This "burning" can possibly point to the burning in the Lake of Fire, the Second Death-**Rev 20:11-15, Mat 25:41-46**

MELCHIZEDEK, JESUS' IMMUTABILITY

Interpretation-God's Promises and Oath

Our Lord Jesus is the anchor of our souls relative to God's **salvation** because of God's two immutable things **(Heb 6:20)**. Because "it is impossible for God to lie" His two immutable things, the heavenly Father's **promises** and God's **oath** to our father Abraham cannot be broken or reversed (**Heb 6:13-14, 6:18).** These immutable things were fulfilled in our Lord Jesus, who is the **promised Seed** and who God raised from the dead because of the **oath (Gal 3:16, Heb 7:20-12).** Thus, through our Lord Jesus being the High Priest who died for us and was raised from the dead, we have "fled for refuge" into the holy of holies (behind the veil). We have fled to the Throne of Grace in the City of Refuge, New Jerusalem, through which we are anchored and free from the pursuit of the avenger of Death. This refuge and anchor we have for our souls is the **sure salvation** through our Lord Jesus Christ according to the order of Melchizedek, "into the age" where Jesus now resides in the right hand of God, being the High Priest over our great and eternal salvation.

Hebrews 6:9-Better Things

Yet, beloved, we are persuaded of **'better-government'** things of you, **and holds of-salvation,** though we speak **in-this-way**.

1. Better is the Greek word "kreíttōn" and is also defined as "stronger," and "what is improved because more fully developed, i.e. in reaching the needed dominion (mastery, dominance)" (see Strong's #2909 and BibleHub.com). The Greek word for better, kreitton, is from "krátos," "dominion," rule, government,

governmental. Thus, better can be defined as dominion, mastery, government, better after dominating (i.e., controlling), stronger, more excellent, and so on.

2. The better-governmental things and "holds" of Salvation represents the things of the Great Salvation, the things of the Eternal Salvation.

a. In **Hebrews 2:3, "great"** (related to **"great salvation"** is translated from the Greek word "telikoutos"—**Strong's #5082.** Telikoutos" is a compound Greek word ho-helikos-houtos, and it literally means "the-adult-**this."** **Here are the Greek words that make up the word "telikoutos," "ho,"** which means "the" in English, plus "helikos," which means "full grown" in English and "houtos" which means "this" in English. Telikoutos is then translated as **"the, adult, this," or rather this the adult, or this the full grown.**

b. Thus, God's salvation plan for mankind also includes the "great" salvation or the "full grown" salvation.

   i. God's great salvation includes the corporate "one new man," in Christ, who has matured into God's "goal" of being conformed "into the Son's image and likeness" to rule the earth **(Rom 8:29, Heb 2:1-10)**

   ii. This salvation is for the those who have grown up (matured) in the order of Melchizedek, matured to become Lord of all in this life and the next millennium **(Gal 4:1-7, Heb 2:1-10, Rev 20:1-6)**

   iii. This "Great Salvation" is then defined as the "Adult Salvation." This is God's salvation for the matured corporate body of Christ (the matured corporate man of love and mature man of proper speech, through which God "under arrange" the world to come under this "adult man," God's matured sons crowned with glory and honor, also called the matured "corporate man" in Christ made up of Jews and Gentiles (**Heb 2:5-10, Eph 4:13, Eph 2:15**).

1. In the next millennium, the fallen angels will not continue to rule over the kingdoms of the habitable world **(Heb 2:5, Luke 4:5-6)**
2. **In the next millennium,** the fallen angels will **<u>not</u>** continue to rule over the kingdom of the world and the glory of them **(Matt 4:8-9).**
3. In conjunction with our Lord Jesus, His wise adult sons will judge the world (**1 Cor 6, Rev 20:1-6).**
4. In conjunction with our Lord Jesus, His wise adult sons will judge angels **(1 Cor 6, Rev 20:1-6).**
5. In conjunction with our Lord Jesus, His wise adult sons will put all enemies under their feet **(Heb 2:1-10, 1 Cor 15:25-28, Rev 20:1-6).**
6. In conjunction with our Lord Jesus, His wise adult sons will rule over "the works of God's hands" (including "the heavens") **(Heb 1:7 w/Heb 2:7).**

c. The great salvation or full-grown salvation also includes the eternal salvation **(Heb 5:9)**. This salvation, (the eternal/full grown) for those who "see" the Lord "welcoming" Him "out of the Second, and "spaced from sin" **(Heb 9:28)**.

d. One of the facets of "maturity" is to have no more consciousness of sins through the sprinkling of the blood of our Lord Jesus in your heart **(Heb 9:14, Heb 10:1-4, Heb 10:16-22)**.

Hebrews 6:10-Ministering to the Lord's Name

Because God is not unrighteous to forget your work and **labor** of **love,** which you **have showed toward his name,** in that you have **minister to-the** saints, and **are-ministering**.

1. This is an important principle to know, ministering to God's saints, is the same as showing love towards His Name.
2. Saying it another way, we demonstrate we love the living God when we love our brothers and sisters (**1 John 4:20).**
3. The Melchizedek order is God's priesthood that minister to both God and their fellow priest-brothers and priest-sisters.
   a. The pattern of the Melchizedek ministry is a ministry that blesses **both** God, the Highest, and blesses those considered God's friends like Abraham (**Gen 14:18-20).**
      i. Disciples who do what the Lord Jesus commands them to do are His **friends (John 15:14-15).**

Hebrews 6:11-12-Fully Wearing Hope

[11]And we **desire** that every one of you do show the same **'speed' towards the 'full-burden-wearing' of-the 'expectation' until** the **'completion.'** [12]That you be not **'lazy,'** but **imitators** of them who through faith and **'longsuffering'** inherit the promises.

1. The saints are to use "speed" in fully wearing the "hope" (lit., expectation) of the resurrection, the hope of eternal life, the hope of the Lord Jesus' return, etcetera, until the completion when the Lord Jesus arrives.
2. That is, we are not to be "lazy" but use "speed" to be imitators of those who inherit God's promises through faith and longsuffering.

a. Longsuffering literally means to be "long to anger;" thus saints are not to get angry when our faith is tested and the hope of Jesus' return or expectation of His help towards us seems to extend beyond our reasoning.

3. It takes both "faith" and "longsuffering" to inherit God's promises. Here are some of God's promises[8]
   a. The promise of Jesus' return (**Heb 10:36-37, 2 Pet 2:4**)
   b. The promise of salvation for nations (**Gal 3:7-8; 3:14**).
   c. The promise of the coming of Heavenly Jerusalem (**Heb 11:9-10**)
   d. The promise of receiving the Holy Spirit (**Gal 3:14, Luke 24:49, Acts 1:4, Acts 2:23, Eph 1:13**).
   e. The promise of God's children (Jews and Gentiles) being heir of the World (**Rom 4:13**)
   f. The Promise of Sonship, being placed as sons like the Lord Jesus (**Gal 3:29 w/Ga; 3:26-29**).
   g. The promise of eternal Inheritance (**Heb 9:15**)
   h. The promise of entering in God's Sabbath Day, the present rest in Christ through faith and the Millennium rest after the first resurrection (**Heb 4:1-11, Rev 20:4-6**)

Hebrews 6:13-God Swore by Himself

Because when God made promise to Abraham, because he could swear by **no greater,** he swore **by himself.**

1. God made a promise to Abraham which is unbreakable (**Heb 6:18**)
2. God's swearing is God's oath that can never be broken (**Heb 6:18**)

---

[8] This list of Promises is not exhaustive

3. God swore by Himself; and by doing this, God showed the immutability of the promise by taking an oath.
4. God swore by Himself, because an oath is the end of all disputes, with the understanding that "dispute" is translated from the Greek word "antilogias," which can be better translated as anti-word, as in being against the word of God.
   a. Anyone who is "anti;" anti-God's word, anti-Christ, anti-Jesus, anti-Christ-likeness will be proved wrong because God's oath related to His promises is sure to His people (**see 2 Thes 2:4 w/2 Thes 2:8 for the end of all anti-God entities).**
5. God swore by Himself, which means that God's "oath" is confirmation of the promises He made with Abraham. There is none who is greater than the living God! There is none greater that God who can reverse God's oath.

Hebrews 6:14-Blessings and Multiplication
Saying, **truly, blessing** I will bless you, and **multiplying** I will multiply you.

1. The oath of God blessed Abraham and multiplied Abraham. Thus, God's oath is life-producing.
2. Bless is the Greek word "eulogos," which mean well-words, good-words.
   a. Those (we) who are of "faith" are "blessed with faithful Abraham (**Gal 3:8)**
   b. We (God's sons and daughters) are blessed with all spiritual "good-words" in the heavenly places in Christ (**Eph 1:4)**
3. God multiplied Abraham' seed, both the seed of Israel according to the flesh and the seed of "the Israel of God"

(His Church) according to the Spirit (**Rom 4:13-17, Rom 9:1-9, Gal 4:21-32**).

Hebrews 6:15-Obtaining the Promise
And so, after he had **long suffered**, he **obtained the** promise.

1. One of the signs that God would fulfill to Abraham all the promises (plural), especially the promise related to God saving the believing Gentiles through "the Seed," the Lord Jesus Christ, is that before Abraham died, Abraham obtained the "promise" of Isaac, the promised seed, who foreshowed, the Promised Seed (Christ) (**Rom 9:8-10, Gal 3:16**).
   a. The Lord Jesus does the same for us; He will fulfill certain promises made to us, in this life, as we wait for the other eternal promises. For example, the promise of the Spirit is given to us as a gift upon request to the heavenly father through faith in Jesus (**Gal 3:14, Luke 24:49, Acts 1:4, Acts 2:23, Eph 1:13, Luke 11:9-13**)

Hebrews 6:16-17-God Unbreakable Oath
[16]Because men **indeed** swear by the **greater,** and an oath for **stabilization** is **to-them** an **end** of all **anti-word**. [17]**In which** God, **counseling-himself more-abundantly** to show **to-the** heirs of promise the **immutability** of his **counsel, mediated** it by an **oath.**

1. Men swear by a greater one than themselves to bring stability and to bring an end to disputes.
2. However, God's willingness to show the heirs (Jews and Gentiles believers in Christ) of the promises the "immutability" of his "plan-counsel" mediated with an oath.

3. Through God's oath and promises, we have a "forceful consolation" related to our salvation **(Heb 6:18). There is no force greater than the living God who created force.**

4. Because of God's promises and oath, we can now flee for refuge behind the veil, into the Holy of Holies (**Heb 6:20**).

Hebrews 6:18-Two Immutable Practices

That by two immutable **practices**, in which **impossible** for God to **lie,** we might have a **'forceful' consolation**, who have **fled for refuge** 'to-government of-the before-laid expectation.'

1. The two immutable practices of God are God's oaths and God's promises which are unchangeable.

2. God's two immutable practices, God's oaths and promises are not lies! God is not a man that He should lie (**Numbers 23:19**). God cannot lie (**Titus 1:2**).

3. God's oath and promises to have a "forceful consolation" (to call beside) related to our safety in His refuge.

4. We who believe in the Lord Jesus Christ have "fled for refuge" into the Most Holy Place, which alludes to the "Cities of Refuge" God instituted through Moses and Joshua.

    a. Six cities were established as refuge cities for a person who killed anyone to flee to from the avenger of bloodshed (family member of the killed). These cities were used for safety of the accused until the accused was judged by the congregation.

        i. The "avenger of blood" can be a relative of a person who was slain who under the law of the Old Covenant is allowed to avenge the killing of a relative, if the accused is found guilty.

   ii. The slayer (refugee) is to be judged by the congregation **according to the writing of Numbers 35:11-15, Joshua 20:2, Joshua 21:27-32, and Deuteronomy 19:1-12**

      1. When the congregation judges the refugee, the question must be answered, was the killing premeditated, was the killing accidental, or unknowingly?

      2. If the slayer is judged by the "congregation" and found not guilty, he is free from punishment. Likewise, we are free from the law (the avenger) of sin and death through the Body of Christ (Jesus' Congregation) (**Rom 7:4).**

   iii. The slayer must remain in a City of Refuge until High Priest dies. Upon death of the High Priest, the slayer is freed (**Num 35:11-15, Josua 20:2, 21:27-32)**

      1. We will live and be free (not put to death by the avenger, Satan) because of the death of our High-Priest, the Lord Jesus on our behalf.

      2. Jesus our High Priest who rose again from the dead eternally delivers us from the avenger of death (**1 John 3:8, Heb 2:14-18)**

      3. Our place of refuge we flee to is behind the veil, where our forerunner, Jesus, our Hight Priest according to the order of Melchizedek have entered ahead of us (**Heb 6:20)**

Hebrews 6:19-Anchor of Our Soul

Which we have as an **anchor of the soul**, both 'certain' and 'stable,' and which enters into **that 'interior' of-the** veil.

1. The "anchor of the soul" is God's oath and God's promises which are immutable, and we access the promises of God through faith in the Lord Jesus and by the Holy Spirit (**Heb 6:17-18, Eph 2:18, Gal 3:14**).
2. Anchor of the soul is the surety of seeing the hope of Jesus Christ; because God's oath and promises cannot lie (**Heb 6:19, Rom 8:23-25**).
3. God's promises and oath is the "certainty" and "stability" of our soul (**Heb 6:18-19**).
4. The anchor of the soul (God's promises and oath) enters into "that" within the veil.
   a. "That within the veil" is "that 'interior' behind the veil" of the Tabernacle in heaven.
   b. "That within the veil" is the High-Priest, Christ, and His offering (**Heb 9:28**).
   c. "That within the veil" is the High-Priest, Jesus' sprinkled blood and Jesus, Himself, the "freshly slain sacrifice" (**Heb 10:19-21, Rev 5:6**).
   d. "That within the veil" is Gold Censer, Gold Altar of Incense, the Ark of the Covenant, the gold pot with the hidden manna, Aaron's rod that budded, the Tables of the Covenant, the cherubs of glory, and the Mercy Seat (**Heb 9:3-5, Rev 2:17, Rev 8:3-5, Rev 15:5-6, etc.**)[9]

Hebrews 6:20-Jesus, the Forerunner
Where the **forerunner, over** us, entered, even Jesus, **became High Priest into the age according** to the **order** of Melchizedek.

---

[9] Please refer to my book *Melchizedek* for exegete of "that within the veil" relative to **Heb 9:3-5 w/Heb 6:20**

1. Forerunner literally means before-racer, before runner, to run ahead, to scout out by going before others.

    a. The Lord Jesus ran the race ahead of us as a forerunner into the holy of holies, entering behind the veil (**Heb 6:19**). We are to follow Jesus our forerunner into the promises.

    b. The "interior of the veil" that the Lord Jesus ran ahead into also includes entering "into the age," the eternal age (**Heb 6:19 w/Heb 6:20**)

2. The phrase "according to" is translated from the Greek word "kata." "Kata" means down from (i.e., moving from a higher plane to a lower plane with special reference to terminus (end point) (J. Thayer).

    a. Thus, the Melchizedek ministry comes down from a higher place (the Highest God) to bring things pertaining to God in the lower plane (the earth)

3. Order is the Greek word "taxis," and it is a military term which means to arrange, "an ordered troop" arranged in descending ranks.

    a. There is the "order" of Melchizedek priesthood functioning in their "portion" or rank of offering "incense" (prayer) to the living God (**Luke 1:8-9, Heb 5:6-7, Ps 141:2, Rev 5:8, Rev 8:3-5**).

    b. There is the Melchizedek priestly "order" of functioning in the gifts of the Holy Spirit, especially relative to speaking in tongues, prophecy, interpretation of tongues, etc. (**1 Cor 14:40 w/1 Cor 14**).

    c. There is the "order' of the Melchizedek priesthood related to remaining steadfast in the faith (**Col 2:5**). That is, in the Melchizedek order we walk by faith and not by sight (**2 Cor 5:7, Heb 11:5-6**).

4. The "Order of Melchizedek" are as follows, and as previously outlined in **Hebrews 5:6** with additional notes. The phrase "order of Melchizedek" is used six (6) or seven (7) times in scriptures depending on which Greek text is used in addition to the Old Testament.

   a. Jesus used **Psalm 110** concerning the order of Melchizedek in reference to His enemies being made His footstool **(Matt 22:41-46).**

   b. The context of all of **Hebrews 5:6** is that of the "calling" of Jesus as God's High Priest is according to the order of Melchizedek.

   c. **Hebrews 5:9-10** is a reference to the Melchizedek order of Jesus being called to public places, not just having Church in a building.

   d. **Hebrews 6:20** references the order of Jesus according to the Melchizedek order as our forerunner into the Holy of Holies, where also we have a refuge for an anchor for souls.

   e. **Hebrews 7:11** references the order of Jesus who is now the Lawgiver that leads us to maturity, according to the order of Melchizedek.

   f. The sixth mention of Jesus order according to Melchizedek relates to Jesus being the High "priest forever."

MELCHIZEDEK BY TRANSLATION

Interpretation-Minding God's Difficult Things

The Lord Jesus, through His holy Spirit have given us a way to understand the "difficult things" of Melchizedek's order as they relate to the Lord Jesus and His Church. Per the great apostle Peter, understanding difficult things are reserved for Jesus disciples (those who study and learn) and those who are stabilized through Jesus Christ **(2 Peter 3:15-16)**. The Lord Jesus' disciples can begin to understand Jesus' High Priest by the "translation" of Melchizedek's name. We can understand Jesus' High Priest by the translation of the words associated with Melchizedek. We can understand Jesus' High Priest by the translation of the city associated with Melchizedek. We can understand Jesus' High Priest by the translation of what is unsaid about Melchizedek (i.e., no mention of being fathered, mothered, no genealogy). This teaching concerning Jesus' more excellent ministry according to the order of Melchizedek is part of the mystery of Christ that was hidden in God until after Jesus came in the flesh some two thousand years ago. The mystery of Jesus and Melchizedek was hidden from angels, generations, ages, etc. However, this mystery of Christ and His Church relative to Melchizedek and his priesthood is only revealed by the Holy Spirit interpretation, comparing spiritual things with spiritual things **(1 Corinthians 2, Eph 3:5, Heb 9:8).**

Hebrews 7:1-King Melchizedek Defined

For this **Melchizedek,** king of **Salem,** priest of the **Highest** God, who **met** Abraham returning from the **slaughter** of the kings and **blessed** him.

1. Melchizedek is defined as King of Righteousness. Melchizedek is a compound word Melek (king) and

Zadok (righteousness). We will look at each word independently.

2. Melek is the Hebrew word translated as "king."
   a. The Lord Jesus taught and exemplified that "kings" are to "serve" the people as Jesus, Himself, as the King, served people (**Luke 22:27 w/Luke 22:24-27**)
   b. The Lord Jesus definition of "kings" is "one who serves" ["diakonon," run errands by kicking up dust)] and "as one who is the younger" ["neoteroi," youth with initiative to lend a hand (**Acts 5:6, Luke 22:24-27**)
   c. Kings are also defined as those who counsel or advise (**Nehimiah 5:1-13, Dan 4:27**). The words translated as "consulted" in **Nehamiah 5:7** is the Hebrew word for "king" (malak). The Aramaic equivalent word for "king" (melek) **is also used in Dan 4:27, translated as "counsel."**
   d. According to Daniel use of the word melek, a King is one who advises to break sins "in" righteousness (**Dan 4:27**). In like manner, King Jesus broke off our sins and brought in everlasting righteousness (**Dan 9:24**).
   e. A king (melek) is one who is to shows mercy to the poor (**Dan 4:27, Neh 5:1-13**). King Jesus saves us by His mercy (**Eph 2:4-7**)
   f. A king (malak) does not charge interest on loans (**Neh 5:1-13**). King Jesus forgives our debts with no interest charged (no remembrance of our debt of sins).
   g. A righteous King (malak) is one who does not buy and sell his brothers, his fellow humans (**Nehamiah 5:1-13 w/Deuteronomy 24:7 w/1 Timothy 1:10**). The penalty of enslaving others is death (**Deuteronomy 24:7**). The Lord Jesus freed us from all slavery-**see (Gal 4, Rom 6, Rom 8, 1 Cor 7:23)**

   h. A king (malak) is one who does not take lands from others **(Neh 5:1-13)**.

3. Zedek is the Hebrew word for "righteousness" as stated earlier.

   a. "Zedek" represents the "Zadok" priesthood who does not go astray from God with idols (covetousness) **(Ezekiel 44, Eph 5:5)**.

   b. Zadok priests are not men-pleasers, rather they are God-pleasers **(Ezekiel 44:7-8, Eph 6:6, Col 3:22)**.

   c. Zadok priests does not "harass" God's holy things or God's holy people **(Ezekiel 44:13)**.

   d. Zadok priests are **not** restricted from ministering to the Lord the bread, the fat, and the blood at His "table"-**Ezekiel 44:15-16**.

      i. The Bread represents the body of Jesus that was broken for us **(1 Cor 11:23-24)**.

      ii. Fat is defined as milk, and also that which conceals the heart, according to the Hebrew pictograph.

      iii. The blood we minister to God is the better blood of Jesus **(1 Cor 11:25-26, Heb 12:24)**.

         1. We constantly thank the Father for the better blood of Jesus that speaks forgiveness.

   e. Zadok priests, due to their faithfulness to the Lord, are rewarded with better resurrection relatively to the intensity of glory, and positionally relative to the concentric circles around God's throne **(Ezekiel 45, 1 Cor 15:41, Rev 5)**.

   f. There is also more New Testament applications to be gleaned of the Melchizedek high priesthood relative to the "Zadok" high priesthood of "Jeshua (Jesus), the son of Jozadak" ("Jehovah is righteous)" in the books of Ezra, Nehamiah, Zachariah, Haggai.

    i. Jeshua, son of Jozakak, was part of the leading men in the restorative work of rebuilding the wall (praise) of Jerusalem (Jesus disciples) and the Temple (God's body of believers filled with the Holy Spirit) also lead by Nehimiah, Ezra, Zerubbabel

4. Melchizedek is the King of Salem, meaning he is King of Peace

    a. Melchizedek was "king of Salem," and not king of Jerusalem (dual and plural in the Hebrew). This was before David conquered Jerusalem to make it the City of God

        i. There is also two Jerusalem (one above and one beneath) (**Gal 4:22-26**).

        ii. Adonizedek was the first mentioned king of Jerusalem beneath. **Note:** he was not king of Salem, as Melchizedek.

            1. Adonizedek was head of the confederate or unionized five (5) kings who were enemies of Gibeon and Joshua (**Joshua 10**)

            2. These five kings' union or confederate represents the false five-fold ministry that are the enemies of the cross of Christ (**Phil 3:17-19, Phil 1:15-18**)

        iii. Adonizedek means Lord of righteousness, socket of righteousness, foundation of righteousness (Strong's #113, #134)

            1. Thus, Adonizedek represents the false "foundation" and therefore false apostles (**2 Cor 11:13-15, contrast Eph 2:19-22**).

            2. Adonizedek is false Melchizedek ministries ministering false righteousness related to earthly pedigree, earthly culture, earthly

ethnicity, earthly nationality (**2 Cor 11:13-15 w/2 Cor 11:18-22 w/Phil 3:1-9, Phil 3:19-20).**

3. Adonizedek is an enemy of Gibeon and Joshua
   a. Adonizedek represents the Sadducees (priests in error) who were the enemies of the greater Joshua (the Lord Jesus our Melchizedek) resurrection, etc. **(Matt 22, Matt 16).**
   b. Adonizedek is the enemy of Gibeon (hilly), where Gibeon can represent the hill Golgotha where our Lord was crucified (the principle of bearing one's cross).
4. Adonizedek is listed as king of Jerusalem, not king of Salam (**Josh 10:1**). **That is,** before king David conquered Jerusalem (formerly Jebus) and made it the City of David, Jerusalem was ruled through false lords of righteousness like Adonizedek (**1 Chron 11:4-5**).

iv. In the New Testament, "New Jerusalem" is properly defined as New Priest-Salem (**Rev 21**)
   1. That is, the Greek word for Jerusalem is "Hierousalem," from the Greek words hierou (priest, sacred, temple) and salem (peace)- **Strong's 2419, BibleHub.com**
      a. Thus, New Jerusalem means New Priest-Peace, New Sacred Peace, New Temple Peace. This is the new "Salem" for Jesus' Melchizedek priesthood.

5. Melchizedek is a Priest of the Highest God which prefigures the exalted Lord Jesus, the High Priest

according to the order of Melchizedek, who is in God's right hand higher than the heaven **(Heb 7:25, Heb 1:3)**.

a. Highest is defined as the upmost in position of absolute ownership and authority to grant conquest **(Gen 14:19-20)**.

b. The Lord Jesus is in God's right hand in the heavens far above all (highest above all) principalities, powers, authorities, world-governments, spiritual hurts in heavens, thrones, lords **(Eph 1:20-23)**.

c. A principle of the "highest God" is that the living God is possessor (absolute Owner) of heaven and earth **(Gen 14:19-20)**.

d. Another principle of the "highest God" is that God delivers our enemies into our hands **(Gen 14:19-20)**.

e. Our Melchizedek High Priest, the Lord Jesus ascended far above all heaven that He may fill all things **(Eph 4:8-10)**.

   i. In Jesus' ascending on high (His Highness, His absolute authority) He captured captivity. This "captivity" that the Lord Jesus "captured" appears to refer to the Lord Jesus capturing principalities and authorities having divested them of their abilities to captivate **(Col 2:15, John 16:11, John 12:31)**. That is, the word captivate is from a compound Greek word that means to be taken by spear **(Strong's #602, #164)**.

   ii. Our Melchizedek High Priest, Jesus, is Higher than the heavens **(Heb 7:26)**. The Lord Jesus is Lord of all that is beneath Him in His place of height **(Phil 2:9-11)!**

   iii. The Melchizedek ministry of Jesus' priesthood sees God as the Highest in the face of war and in the defeating of our enemies **(Gen 14:20).**

6. Melchizedek being the Priest of the Highest, prefigures our Lord Jesus the Son of the Highest. This truth of the Lord Jesus being the Son of the Highest torments demons to manifest and empowers us to cast out demons from people **(Luke 8:28)**

   i. God, the Highest, gives us dominion over demons and/or Satan's angels now and in the millennium **(Luke 10:17-20, Rev 20:1-3)**

   ii. Jesus bound Satan when he came in the flesh the first time; and Satan will be bound again in the abyss when the Lord Jesus returns in His coming **(Rev 20:1-3, Mat 12:28-29)**

   iii. Satan's angels/demons are also judged and bound from the earth-**Rev 20:1-3, Mat 12:28-29, John 16:11, John 12:31).**

7. Melchizedek was a king and priest representing the Lord Jesus' Kingship and Priesthood.

   i. That is Melchizedek prefigured Jesus, our King and Jesus our High-Priest **(Matt 2:2, John 18:37). In John 18:37,** the Lord defined His Kingship as the Truth!

   ii. The Lord's Melchizedek ministry also consists of His corporate kingly priesthood. This is royal priesthood of believer apostle Peter spoke of also calling them a holy priesthood **(1 Pet 2:9, 1 Pet 2:6).** We will discuss later the corporate priesthood as **the** "priest-togetherness."

iii. Melchizedek, the king priest also represents the King-Priest, Jesus and his kings and priests continuing to rule the habitable world after the first Resurrection (**Rev 20:1-6, Heb 2:1-10)**

iv. The Melchizedek kingly priesthood can also be understood in Jesus' twenty-four (24) Elders of kings-priests mentioned in **Revelation 4:4.**

    1. There are twenty-four (24) division of the order (courses) of the priesthood as the Spirit of the Lord revealed to David through writings (**1 Chronicles 24 w/1 Chronicles 28:19)**

    2. Therefore, twenty-four (24) is symbolic of priesthood.

v. The twenty-four (24) Elders sat on thrones (seats) with victor's crowns. Therefore, like their King Jesus, they are also kings of the Melchizedek order. The twenty-four (24) Elders are also called "lords" Therefore they are matured placed sons as joint heir with Christ, which **Galatians 4:1-7** defines as such (**Rev 7:13-14, Gal 4:1, Rev 19:16).**

vi. The 24 Elders represent Jesus' Melchizedek priesthood as "seniors," "mature men with seasoned judgment. Thus, on their thrones as kings and priest, they are matured "counselors" (a previously discussed definition of a king (for the definition of "elders," see Strong's #4245, BibleHub.com)

vii. Thus, the twenty-four (24) Elders with twenty-four (24) crowns and twenty-four (24) seats (thrones) represent the mature Melchizedek kingly priesthood of Jesus Christ (**1 Pet 2:9, Rev 4:4, Rev 20-4-6).**

1. See **Heb 7:11; 7:12; 7:24** where "priesthood" is literally "priest togetherness" formed from hieros (priest) and sun (together, with).
2. That is, we are priests together with our High-Priest, Jesus Christ!

8. Melchizedek met Abraham returning from the slaughter of the kings.
   a. Thus, Melchizedek originally "met" Abraham on earth. It is established that the Lord Jesus met us on earth giving us His bread (His body) and His wine (His blood) so may live by Him and remember Him **(John 6:22-63, 1 Cor 11:23-28)**
   b. Melchizedek met Abraham when Abraham was uncircumcised. Thus, the Melchizedek ministry is also to the uncircumcised, the Gentile nations **(Rom 4:9-17, etc.)**
   c. The word translated as "met" when Melchizedek met Abraham means "together-apposite," therefore face to face. The Lord Jesus, our Melchizedek, will meet face to face with the first resurrection saints, who are and will be kings-priests on earth (**1 Cor 15:23, 1 Thes 4:13-18**, **Rev 20:1-6). Also,** in being resurrected kings and priests, we will also be meeting face to face with the generations of the next millennium as part of our function.
   d. The first resurrection saints, starting in the next millennium will be able to migrate between the visible and invisible like our resurrected Lord Jesus (**Luke 23:31 w/Luke 23:15).**

9. Melchizedek met Abraham when Abraham was returning from the slaughter of the kings.
   a. Slaughter also means a cutting. Thus, during the war that Abraham fought against the kings, there was

literal "cutting" where blood was shed in the war. The point in knowing this is that it did not disqualify Abraham from partaking of communion (partaking of the bread and wine) with Melchizedek.

b. Yes, Melchizedek ministered or gave bread and wine to Abraham after the slaughter (**Gen 14:18).**

    i. Thus, bloodshed in war, or through military purposes or orders, does not disqualify a brother or sister in the Lord Jesus from having communion to partake of inner healing in the conscience. There is a difference between shedding blood in peace and shedding blood in war, even though God does not sanction shedding human blood (**1 Kings 2:5 and Gen 9:3-6).**

    ii. This principle of Melchizedek and Abraham having communion after the slaughter of the kings also points to the principle of having communion with the Lord Jesus in His kingdom after the slaughter of the beast, the slaughter of the false prophet and the slaughter of the beast's armies (**Mat 26:26-29, Rev 19:9-21).**

c. The Melchizedek priesthood involves war against God's enemies (**Psalm 110, Rev 19, Heb 10:13, Gen 14:18-21, etc.)**

    i. King Jesus' conquest of the three beasts will be accomplished through "sharp sword" of Jesus' mouth, not manmade weapons **(Rev 19:15).**

        1. The three beasts, to include, but not limited to the man of lawlessness, etcetera will be "annihilated" through the "Spirit of Jesus' mouth," and in "the brightness of His coming," not natural weapons (**2 Thess 2:8, Dan 8:25)**

2. Christians of Jesus' Melchizedek order do not war with weapons made by flesh (**2 Cor 10:3-4**)

3. Christians of Jesus' Melchizedek order war against our enemies with the spoken Word of God, through the eternal Spirit and spiritual weapons (**Acts 13:9-12, John 18:5-6, Eph 6:10-19**).

10. Melchizedek also blessed Abraham. blessed as defined in the New Testament Greek definitions means "good word."

   a. A blessing of the Highest God is that He possesses heaven and earth. Therefore, God, the Highest, rules in the kingdom of men and He gives it to whom he will (**Dan 4:17**).

   b. God, the Highest, supernaturally delivers our enemies into our hands as He did for Abraham even though Abraham only had three hundred eighteen (318) men fighting against the armies of four kings of four nations (**Gen 14:1-16**)

   c. Abraham tithed after the blessing of Melchizedek. Thus, saints of the Highest God should tithe all the forms of tithing after the Lord Jesus blesses them with His salvation, His Holy Spirit, His love, His sonship, and so on (**Matt 23:23**).

      i. Note: according to the scriptures the forms of tithing consists of tithing justice (judgment), tithing mercy, tithing faith, tithing produce, tithing money, tithing animals (**Matt 23:23, Numbers 18, etc.**).

Hebrews 7:2-Understanding by Translation

To whom also Abraham **tenth from all** parts; **foremost** being by **translation** King of **righteous-togetherness**, and also **King of Salem,** which is, **King of peace.**

1. Abraham tithed to Melchizedek **after Melchizedek blessed** Abraham; and the principle of tithing can be understood by the first context of tithing, the definition of tithing and the hieroglyphics reading of the Hebrew word for tithe.

    a. The first record of tithing was Abraham tithing to Melchizedek.

    b. The first tithe was **"given" voluntarily** before it was legislated (made law). Abraham gave voluntarily after he saw the greatness and maturity of Melchizedek.

    c. Tithe is translated from the Hebrew word spelled "mosher," or "masar," which means "from-accumulation" (Strong's #4642, #6241, #6235

       i. Thus, we tithe from what we accumulate.

    d. Tithe is also defined as "from-riches" another definition for "mosher."

       i. Thus, the rich are also to tithe from their riches.

    e. Tithe is also defined as "from-wealth."

       i. Thus, the wealthy are to tithe from their wealth.

    f. The Hebrew word picture or hieroglyphics understanding for "maser" can be understood as "from seeing the prince," or "from-experiencing-the prince" [(מ) mim (from) and (ע) aiyn (eye, to see) and (שר) sar (prince)].

       i. Therefore, a believer in Christ voluntarily tithes when we "experience" the "Prince," the Lord Jesus, our resurrected High Priest in His "greatness" and exceptional maturity **(Heb 7:4)**

    ii. That is, if we really "experience" Jesus as Lord, our King High Priest, our Savior, our Deliverer, etcetera, we voluntarily give tithe to His Melchizedek order (compare **Luke 8:1-3**).

2. Abraham tithed a tenth, the top, from all the spoils to Melchizedek.

    a. Tithe of all is understood to be the all from first-fruits crops or spoils from the top.

    b. The Greeks usually take from the top-most of a heap to offer to the gods.

3. Per the writer of the book of Hebrews, the Melchizedek ministry is understood **"foremost by translation."** This translation of the words associated with Melchizedek gives insight into the mystery of the Melchizedek order.

    a. It is acknowledged that The Melchizedek mystery is difficult to interpret, lit., difficult to translate **(Heb 5:11)**.

    b. The mystery of Melchizedek is understood foremost by translation as indicated above.

        i. We can understand the mystery of Melchizedek by translation of Melchizedek's **name.**

        ii. We can understand the mystery of Melchizedek by translation of the **words** associated with Melchizedek.

        iii. We can understand the mystery of Melchizedek by translation of the **city** associated with Melchizedek.

        iv. We can understand the mystery of Melchizedek by translation of what is **unsaid** about Melchizedek (for example, there is no mention of Melchizedek being fathered, mothered, or having genealogy).

4. The mention of Abraham's tithing to Melchizedek (translated as King of Righteousness) is not frivol. Tithing

is linked to King Jesus' "righteousness-togetherness" "with" us. That is, one of the acts of righteousness-togetherness is "**giving**" tithe. Yes, tithing is part of the vast ways of giving and receiving **(Heb 7:4 w/Acts 20:35).**

5. Tithing is linked to King Jesus' (Melchizedek's) city, Salem (Peace). That is, the Lord's peace is linked to tithing. There is peace in giving tithe **(see Rom 15:5-7).**

Hebrews 7:3-Melchizedek Similarity
Without-fathered, without-mothered, without-genealogy, having neither **original** of days, nor **finish** of life; **yet from-similar to-the** Son of God; **remains** a priest **into the through-carry**.

1. Melchizedek was made without-father, without-mother, and without-genealogy. Thus, Melchizedek had no natural pedigree to identify with or to be identified by.

   a. Thus, people's ethnic birth does not qualify or disqualify them from becoming a part of the Melchizedek order. The Lord Jesus Christ, through faith in Him, is who qualifies a person to be part of the Melchizedek's order **(1 Tim 1:4).**

   b. Race based priestly genealogy does not qualify or disqualify a person from becoming part of the Melchizedek priesthood. Again, it is the Lord Jesus Christ and faith in Him is who qualifies a person to be part of the Melchizedek's order **(1 Tim 1:4).**

   c. The Melchizedek order is not based on fleshly heritage. Melchizedek (the Lord Jesus) is made High Priest according to the power of an **"indestructible life,"** or **un-loosed-life (Heb 7:14-16).**

2. Melchizedek had no origin of days; he had no end or finish of life.

a. There is no record of Melchizedek's physical birth or death. Therefore, the interpretation of no record of Melchizedek's death existing is that he is still living in the heavens, having been "carried-through" where he remains a priest of God submitted to Jesus' High Priesthood (**Heb 7:8).**

Melchizedek was made like the Son of God.

b. The phrase used of Melchizedek being "made like the Son of God" literally reads as Melchizedek "'from-simulate' the Son of God." That is, Melchizedek's life and ministry "simulated" Jesus, the Son of God.

c. Here are some of the meanings of the term "Son of God."

  i.   The Son of God is the Christ (**John 20:31).**
  ii. The Son of God is the King of Israel (**John 1:49)**
  iii. The Son of God demonstrates ability to walk on water (**Mat 14:28-33)**

d. The Son of God is personified in the matured man ministry. The "matured man" meaning the corporate one new man in Christ who grows up into having the same/oneness of faith and the same/oneness of knowledge of the Son of God (**Eph 4:11-16).**

  i.   Note: having the knowledge and faith of the Son of God will result in saints not being tossed by every wind of doctrine by the deceitfulness and "cube" (guide) of men

  ii. Having the knowledge and faith of the Son of God will result in saints not being deceived by the "methods" of men, with the understanding that the word "deceived" is translated from the Greek word "kybeia" (transliterated as "cube"). This word "kybeia" (cube) is associated with "kybernao," steering, piloting (Strong's #2940, #2941). The deceived is steered away from the road of Christ through humanistic doctrines instead of the doctrine of Christ! The word "method" literally means a "changing of the road" or to "change a mode" of travel.

   iii. Like the Son of God, the Lord Jesus, we are to be true in the faith in love, and in knowledge that edifies **(compare 1 Cor 8:1)**

   iv. Through attaining to Jesus' knowledge and faith, we are to grow up in all things in Christ, the Head

   v. Through attaining to Jesus' knowledge and faith, the Body of Christ is to edify itself in love.

e. Melchizedek simulating the Son of God is demonstrated in Melchizedek's greatness and adulthood.

f. The principle of the "Son of God" is also equivalent to the Lord Jesus, the Great High-Priest **(Heb 4:14).**

g. The name Son of God is the Lord Jesus mature ability to destroy the works (sin) of the Devil **(1 John 3:8)**

h. Being like the Son of God also means having eyes like fire (discerning) **(Rev 2:18)**. Eyes life fire is Jesus' ability to see the hearts of men (deep thoughts and internal angers) and their kidneys (their end) **(Heb 4:12, Rev 2:23, Jeremiah 17:10)**

i. The Son of God also had feet like brass-incense **(Rev 2:18)**

   i. Brass can be understood to mean crucified serpent based on the scriptures and Hebrew Hieroglyphics **(John 3:13-14, Numbers 21:8-9)**

     1. The Hebrew spelling for "brass" is that of nechosheth. It is derived from Hebrew word: "nachash," defined as serpent, divination, the Hebrew letter "tav" at the end. "Tav" means

    cross, or sign. Hence, brass symbolizes Jesus, the crucified-serpent for sin **(John 3:13-14)**

2. Incense is symbolic of prayers, intercession, to judge, etc. **(Rev 5:8, Ps 141:2).**

3. Therefore, Son of God's feet judge serpents and diviners through his crucifixion and intercessory prayers.

j. Son of God is the Lord Jesus, our High Priest carried through into heavens where He is still executing His office as the High Priest **(Heb 4:14)**

k. Son of God is the manifestation of the Lord Jesus loving others and He gave himself for others **(Gal 2:20).**

l. In the Son of God all His promises are yes and amen (so be it) **(2 Cor 1:19).**

m. The demonstration of the Son of God is the Lord Jesus declared to be the Son of God with power and in the Spirit of Holiness-**Rom 1:4**

n. Son of God is demonstrative glory in resurrecting the dead (for example, Jesus' resurrecting Lazarus') **(John 11:4, Luke 7:12-17).**

o. Son of God's voice produces life **(John 5:25).**

p. Son of God being the highest in holiness, authority, power, and so on torments demons **(Luke 8:28).**

q. Preaching Jesus Christ, the Son of God, is the beginning of the gospel **(Mark 1:1).**

r. Melchizedek simulating the Son of God is the Lord Jesus walking with us in the middle of fire we may experience **(Dan 3:25-28).**

    i. Jesus, our Melchizedek, is with us when we are cast in the fiery furnace, or the furnace of affliction because we refuse idolatry and phantom worship **(Dan 3)**

    ii. Jesus, our Melchizedek, is with us in the fire of affliction because we refuse the music related to man's pollution, man's lust, and idol worship (**Dan 3**)

3. Melchizedek remains a "priest into the carried-through." This means that Melchizedek did not die; however, he was transported back (carried through) into heaven.
   a. Like Melchizedek, the Lord Jesus was "carried-through" into the heaven (**John 20:17**)
      i. The Lord Jesus was "carried-through" into the heaven with His Sacrifices. The sacrifices of His blood, His contrite spirit, His broken heart; and He is as the slain Lamb of God.
      ii. The Lord Jesus, our Melchizedek, was carried-through into heaven and sat down in God's righthand after He offered one sacrifice for sin (**Heb 10:12**).
      iii. The Lord Jesus, our High Priest was carried-through into the heavens for those being sanctified through faith in Him (**Heb 10:14**)
         1. **Note:** Those being sanctified through the one sacrifice of the Lord Jesus were also carried-through seated with Him upon-heaven-**Heb 10:14 w/Eph 2:5-6**

Hebrews 7:4-Melchizedek, The Distinguished Adult
Consider 'how-distinguished-adult' this man was, to-whom even the **patriarch** Abraham **gives** tenth **out of** the **'first-portion.'**

1. The word "consider" is the Greek: "theōréō" means to gaze, to contemplate.
2. "Theōréō" is the root word of the English term "theatre" is derived.

a. Theatre is defined as the act of viewing and determining the meaning or purpose of an action in an event or performance.

b. That is, in order to understand the Melchizedek order, we can't casually look at or read what is said of him. We must also contemplate the things related to Melchizedek asking for Holy Spirit revelation.

3. The word "great" used to describe Melchizedek is defined as "how distinguished an adult," Great is from the Greek word "pelikos."

a. "Pelikos" means great, distinguished, large, prime, eminent (see **Gal 6:11, Heb 7:4).**

   i. Pelikos is from "helix"-adult comrade, full grown, grown up, full age, stature, of age, prime (**Strong's #2245, #2244, BibleHub.com, ISA)**

b. The Melchizedek's priesthood is an "adult" priesthood related to God's **"great" salvation** to the "sons of man" who will "grow up" through God to rule the earth with Christ Jesus (**Heb 2:3).**

c. In **Hebrews 2:3,** "great" (in the phrase "great salvation") is translated from the Greek word "telikoutos" (**Strong's #5082).**

   i. "Telikoutos" is a compound Greek word consisting of three words: ho-helikos-houtos, which can be translated as **the-adult-this.**

   ii. Ho (the) and helikos (full grown) and houtos (this)

   iii. **The-adult-this, this the adult, this the full grown**

d. The "great" salvation is the "full grown" salvation.

   i. The great salvation is God's salvation he has for the corporate new man in Christ that has matured into his image to rule the earth.

   ii. This great salvation is for the those who have grown up (matured) in the Melchizedek priesthood imaging the priesthood of the Lord Jesus.

e. Great salvation is also defined as the "adult salvation," which is God's salvation for the matured corporate body of Christ to whom God "under arranged" (subjected) the world to be shepherded by them with the unyielding rod of iron. These are God's sons whom God crowned with glory and honor in resurrection and authority to rule) (**Heb 2:5-10**)

   i. The fallen angels will not continue to rule over the "kingdoms of the habitable-world" **(Heb 2:5, Luke 4:5-6).**

   ii. The fallen angels will not continue to rule over the "kingdom of the world" and the glory of them **(Matt 4:8-9).**

   iii. In concurrence with our Lord Jesus, His wise adult sons will judge the world (**1 Cor 6, Rev 20:1-6**)

   iv. In concurrence with our Lord Jesus, His wise adult sons will judge angels (**1 Cor 6, Rev 20:1-6**).

   v. In concurrence with our Lord Jesus, His wise adult sons will put all enemies under their feet (**Heb 2:1-10, 1 Cor 15:25-28, Rev 20:1-6**).

   vi. In unification with our Lord Jesus, His wise adult sons will rule over "the works of God's hands," the heavens also (**Heb 1:7 w/Heb 2:7**).

f. The great salvation is also the eternal salvation (**Heb 5:9**).

g. This is the "salvation" (eternal/full grown) for those who "see" the Lord "from-welcoming" Him out of the second spaced apart from sin (**Heb 9:28**).

   i. One of the facets of "maturity" is believers growing up not having a consciousness of sins, being freed through the sprinkling of the blood of our Lord Jesus upon our hearts (**Heb 9:14, Heb 10:1-4, <u>Heb 10:16-22)</u>**

4. **Abraham being called a Patriarch means he is a chief-father, a beginning-father.**

   a. Father is defined as founder, and progenitor.

   b. The word "Patriarch" is used of David (**Acts 2:29**).

      i. David, the chief father related to Jesus and Jesus' dad by law, Joseph, and Jesus' mother Mary (**Luke 2:1-4**).

   c. The word "Patriarch" is used of the Twelve Sons of Jacob (**Acts 7:8-9**). **Thes twelve sons are the** chief fathers of Israel called the "circumcision" according to the flesh.

   d. Again, "Patriarch" is used of Abraham (**Heb 7:4**).

      i. Abraham is the beginning father of faith with respect to salvation for all nations ("the Israel of God"), those "uncircumcised" in the flesh, but circumcised by/in the Holy Spirit [**Rom 4:11-17, Rom 2:28-29, Col 2:9-11, compare Acts 3:25** (where the phrase "families" is the Greek word patria, which means fatherhood, one who produce lineage as a progenitor)].

      ii. Abraham is the beginning father of the circumcision, Israel according to the flesh (**Rom 4:11-17**)

   e. **Note:** Spiritual fathers, in the Church of Jesus, exist in every age (**1 Thess 2:11, 1 Tim 5:1, 1 Cor 4:15, Phil 2:22, 1 John 2:13**)

      i. **<u>"Mark"</u>** those who demand to be "called" fathers or make it a dogmatic doctrine to call them fathers, contrary to what our Lord Jesus taught (**Matt 23:9, Phil 3:17**).

1. The great apostle Paul acknowledged "fathers" exists in the ministry of Jesus Christ **(1 Thess 2:11, 1 Cor 4:14)**; however, there is no record of the saints "calling" him "father Paul," or Paul being "called" a father by the saints whom he served in the ministry.

2. On the contrary, apostle Paul emphasized to the **few** men he called "sons" (Timothy, Onesimus and Titus), and apostle Peter to his "son," (Mark), their "genuine birth" and "service" as sons who serve with them in the ministry, rather than demanding to be called fathers, though they are indeed true fathers in the Lord. This is a nuanced understanding, but true **(1 Peter 5:13, Philemon 1:10, 1 Tim 2:1, Phil 2:22, 2 Cor 12:14)**.

5. **Abraham gave a tenth (tithe) to Melchizedek.**
   a. Foremost, **"tithing"** is considered **"giving."**
   b. Tithing is part of the Lord Jesus' teaching about giving and receiving **(Matt 23:23)**.
   c. The Lord Jesus did not abolish tithing **(Matt 23:23)**
   d. The Hebrew word for tithe is "mosher" [(מעשר) mim (מ) and eser (עשר)].
      i. A Hebrew pictograph that can be formed from this word is: "from-seeing (experiencing)-the prince."
      ii. That is, the Hebrew word "eser" (עשר) is made up the letters ayin (ע), a picture of an eye, to see, to experience, to know, and Hebrew letters that is also used for "prince" (שר), shin (ש) and resh (ר).
      iii. "Mim" (מ) used as a prefix in the word for tithe "mosher" (מעשר) means "from." Hence, a Hebrew pictograph of the word "tithe" ["mosher" (מעשר)]

can be interpreted as "tithing is 'from-experiencing-(the)-prince.'"

e. The Hebrew word for tithe is from a root word "eser" (עשר) which by definition means accumulation, wealth, and riches, according to Strong's dictionary.

   i. From whatever amounts we accumulate (a lot or a little), we tithe from our accumulation on hand.

   ii. For those who are rich, they tithe from their riches.

   iii. For those who are wealthy, they tithe from their wealth.

f. Giving of tithe to the Melchizedek priesthood "witnesses" that the Lord Jesus "lives" **(Heb 7:8).**

   i. **Note**: Levi was commanded to take tithe of the people, **their brothers (Heb 7:5).** So, it is right for believer to tither to their brothers and sisters in the five-fold ministry (apostles, prophets, evangelists, pastors, teachers).

   ii. Giving of tithe is now legislated and part of walking in the Melchizedek order maturely, as the patriarch Abraham demonstrated (**Heb 7:5-14**)

   iii. Saying it another way, God's "people" the "brothers" of the five-fold ministers of the Lord Jesus' are to tithe to **Jesus'** true ministers of the gospel.

g. Paul alluded to the giving of tithe to fellow brothers (priest-workers) even if the brother works (**1 Cor 9:6-14).**

   i. Paul, through grace was a "minister," ("people-worker"), "ministering" (lit., "priest-worker") of the gospel of God" **(Rom 15:15-16).**

   ii. God's people are to share all good things to the ones who minister to them by **teaching** them (the word "teach" used in **Galatians 6:6** is the Greek "catechize" and "catechism" which means learning by questions and answers.

6. Abraham gave the first portion to Melchizedek. First-portion is the Greek word "akrothinion," which means the top (of the) heap, first fruits, first portion, spoils. Among the Greeks, it was the topmost part offered to the gods.

    a. As Abraham tithed to Melchizedek from the first fruit of the spoils, and as all Abraham's children in his loins (before the seed was transferred through copulation) also tithed to Melchizedek, so all of Abraham's spiritual children are to tithe to Jesus, our Melchizedek and Jesus' Melchizedek's priesthood **(Heb 7:4 w/Heb 7:9)**.

    b. The principle of giving tithed was also defined by Jacob. As God gives to us, we in turn **willingly** tithe according to the order of Melchizedek priesthood **(Gen 28:22)**

Hebrews 7:5-Understanding Tithing

And **indeed,** they that are **'out of'** the sons of Levi, **'the priesthood receiving,'** have a commandment **to-from-tenth** of the people according to the law, that is, of their **brothers**, though they come out of the loins of Abraham.

1. The Sons of Levi are those whom God chose to serve the tabernacle that Moses built (High Priest, Priests, Levites)

2. The Levitical priests have a "commandment" to take tithe of the people, their brothers.

3. The other sons of Israel tithed to their brother (the priests-workers) even though they have the same father (Abraham)

4. The people of Jesus are to tithe to the preachers, "priest-workers," of the Gospel of Christ even if the minister also works a job not related to the priesthood **(1 Cor 9:1-14).**

a. Apostles Paul and Barnabas worked, yet received money from the people (**1 Cor 9:6**)

    i. Paul, though a priest-worker, also owned a tent making business (**Acts 18:1-3).**

    ii. Paul, though an apostolic priest-worker, also participated in giving and receiving (**Acts 20:33-35, Phil 4:10-23)**

b. Yet, "the Lord **ordained** that those who preach the gospel should live of the gospel" -(**1 Cor 9:14 w/1 Cor 9:9-11**)

    i. **Note:** "ordain," is a Greek compound word from dia (through) and tasso (to order). Therefore, tithing and giving to preachers are part of the "order" of Jesus' Melchizedek ministry.

5. Paul, through grace was a "minister," a "'**priest-worker'** of the gospel of God" (**Rom 15:15-16**)

6. Disciples of Christ is to share all good things to the one who teaches them [note: as previously stated teach is defined as catechize/catechism, learning by questions and answers (Q&A) in **Galatians 6:6**].

a. If those who are being taught does not give to their teachers, it is considered "sowing to the flesh" and they will "reap corruption" (**Gal 6:6-9).**

b. Giving to those who teaches you the word of God is considered "**sowing** to the Spirit" with a "reaping" of eternal life (**Gal 6:6-9). Compare 1 Tim 6:17-19** where giving is again linked to eternal life.

Hebrews 7:6-Blessings and Tithing

Yet, he whose **genealogy** is not **out of**-them 'received-tenth' from Abraham and **blessed** him that had the **promises.**

1. Melchizedek was so distinguished that Abraham tithed to him who was not of the genealogy of Abraham (Levi).

a. This truth, prefigures tithing to the Jesus's Melchizedek's order who is not of the "genealogy" of Levi, but of the "genealogy" of Judah (**Heb 7:13-15**)

2. Melchizedek **blessed** Abraham that had **the promises,** and the Melchizedek's blessing was link to Abraham's willingness to tithe to him.

   a. Bless is the Greek word eulogy ["eu" (good) and "logos" (word).

      i. Melchizedek spoke "good" and "well" "words" over Abraham (**Gen 14:19**)

         1. He said Abraham is "**of** the Highest God."

         2. He blessed Abraham with the knowledge that the Highest God is the "possessor (owner) of heaven and earth."

   b. Melchizedek blessed Abraham who had the Promises.

      i. Abraham is the patriarch of the Promised Seed, Christ (**Gal 3:16**)

      ii. One of God's promises is the Promised Holy Spirit to be given to believers in Jesus Christ (**Gal 3:14**)

      iii. God promised Justification for the nations, through the Seed, Jesus Christ (**Gal 3:7-9**).

      iv. The "City" (father land) is the land of promise (**Heb 11:9-16). This City is New Jerusalem.**

      v. All the promises of God in Jesus Christ are yes and amen (**2 Cor 1:19-22**)

   c. Melchizedek blessed Abraham [therefore all the seed of Abraham in his loins (those of the law and those of faith are also blessed)] (**Rom 4:13-17**).

      i. Levi and all the tribes were in Abraham loins when he was blessed (**Heb 7:10**)

      ii. All future children of fathers (after their passing) can be blessed with same blessing the father received, even though they don't physically see the children (**Hos 12:4**)

    1. So likewise, the seed of faith also were blessed by Melchizedek in Abraham.

    2. **Note**: Jesus, the Seed, was not transferred to Mary by man.

    3. So how was the promised Seed planted? By the "sperm" of God's "rhema"[10] Word and the Holy Spirit (**Luke 1:34-38**).

  d. Abraham tithed to Melchizedek after Melchizedek's blessed him.

    i. Preachers are not authorized to curse God's people to get money (**Gal 3:13-14**).

    ii. We are no longer under the curse of the law; thus, the curse o**f Malachi 3:8-9** related to tithing does **not** apply to Jesus' priesthood (**Gal 3:13-14**).

    iii. In the days of Moses, the "rock" that produced water was the spiritual Rock, Christ (**1 Cor 10:4**).

      1. Thus, preachers cannot "smite" Christ, "the Rock," twice, as Moses mistakenly did.

        a. There is Jesus, the Christ (**Matt 16:16**).

        b. There is also the Corporate Christ made up believers who are baptized in the Holy Spirit (**1 Cor 12:12**).

      2. Moses was commanded to smite the rock the first time (**Ex 17:16**); and he was commanded to only "speak" to the rock the second time (**Num 20:8**).

      3. That is, the Lord Jesus Christ was smitten (cursed) once on the cross. The "corporate"

---

[10] "Rhema" by definition means, among other things, **words from a living person,** God's spoken words, declarations

Christ consisting of His Body of believers are not to be smitten (cursed) by preachers a second time in order to get tithe (**Gal 3:13-14, James 3:8-12**).

4. Saying it another way, we are not supposed to smite Christ (His corporate Body, His Church) a second time with curses in order to get money or spiritual water out of them.

5. Moses could not enter into the promised land for smiting the Rock (Christ) a second time; so likewise, preachers who smite the corporate Christ may not see certain promises for not "believing" the Lord would provide the water or money. This smiting of the Rock twice is called not "sanctifying the Lord" in the sight of the people (**Num 20:11-12**).

Hebrews 7:7-Blessed of the Better

Yet, without all **anti-word,** the **inferior** is blessed **under** the **better-government.**

1. Abraham was inferior to Melchizedek.
   a. Abraham was blessed "under" a better-government, the government of the "order of Melchizedek."
   b. We are inferior (subject to) the Lord Jesus Christ and are blessed by Jesus' better governmental heavenly blessings (**Eph 1:3-5**).
      i. One of the heavenly blessings in Christ is that God has predestined us to become "sons" like the Lord Jesus and to become "placed-son" like our Lord Jesus (**Gal 4:1-7, Rom 8:23**).
2. Melchizedek functioned in a "better-government."
   a. Melchizedek functioned in the better government of the Highest God

     i. Melchizedek understood that the Highest God owns (governs) everything the heavenly Father created (every creature and/or created thing) in all the heavens, on all the earth, under the earth and in all the seas.

3. The word "better" is the Greek word "kreitton;" and it means stronger, more excellent. It is from "kratos," which means government, rule, dominion, strong, etc.

   a. "Kratos" is transliterated "cracy," think of "democracy," "demo" which means people and "cracy," rule, government.

   b. The Melchizedek order's better-government is a government of "Theocracy" (God-rule).

4. Melchizedek was better in dominion through the government of the Highest God, so likewise the Lord Jessus' Melchizedek priesthood.

   a. God, the Highest "better-government," owns everything and we are joint-heirs with Christ (**Gen 14:18-20, Rom 8:17**)

   b. God, the Highest better-dominion," delivers our enemies into our hands (**Gen 14:18-20 w/Rev 20:1-3**).

   c. Jesus, the High Priest of the Highest, administers "better" life (eternal life) through communion (Jesus' bread and wine) (**Gen 14:18-20 w/1 Cor 11:23-34 w/John 6**)

   d. Jesus, the High Priest of the Highest, administer His "better" blood that speaks forgiveness (**Heb 12:24**)

   e. In Jesus' Melchizedek's order there are better governmental promises, better government resurrection, better governed father-land, better-governed Covenant, and so on.

Hebrews 7:8-The Witness that Jesus Lives

And **here** men that **die takes** tithes; **yet** there he of whom it is **witnessed** that he **lives**.

1. Here (in this life) men that die take tithe.
2. There, when Abraham was living on earth, Abraham tithe to Melchizedek who it is witnessed that Melchizedek is still living.
   a. If tithing was commanded to be given to men that die, why are men and women discounting tithing towards Jesus and His priests of whom it is witnessed that the Lord Jesus is alive (**Mat 23:23, Heb 7:8, Matt 28:6, Luke 24:6**)
      i. Tithing to Jesus, the Melchizedek, witnesses that Jesus is alive with flesh and bone body (**Luke 24:39**)
3. Tithing was established by Abraham and Jacob before it was also legislated. Thus, tithing is a practice of faith towards God for his provision to us and His protection of us (**Gen 14:18-20, Gen 28:20-22**)

Hebrews 7:9-10-The Loins of Abraham

[9]And as I may so say, **Levi also**, who **takes** tithes, **has-tenth through** Abraham. [10]Because, he was yet in the **loins of his father**, when Melchizedek **together-meet** him.

1. Levi and all twelve tribes tithed to Melchizedek through Abraham, their patriarch, and our patriarch through faith.
   a. Levi and his brothers also tithed to Melchizedek "because, [Levi] was yet in the loins of his father [Abraham] when Melchizedek met him."
2. Levi and all the sons of Israel were in Abraham's loins, before the seed was transferred to Isaac through Sarah

a. With that said, all the seed of Abraham were in his loins [those of the law and those of faith (**Hos 12:4, Rom 4:13-17**)].

3. Thus, one of the emphases of this referenced text **(Hebrews 7:9-10)** is to show how great Melchizedek was in that **"all"** (Abraham and all those in Abraham's loins) tithed to Melchizedek.

a. Thus, we are to respect the Lord Jesus Christ in the same way, for conscience's sake, by tithing/giving to His Melchizedek order of priesthood.

MELCHIZEDEK, OF THE TRIBE OF JUDAH

Interpretation-From Levi to Judah

One of the difficult things for the Hebrew Christians to believe during in the days of Jesus, Peter, John, Paul, Barnabas, Timothy, Silas, and so on, was to believe that the priesthood was changed from Levi to Judah. This truth was part of God's hidden wisdom and one of God's hidden mysteries concerning Jesus, the Christ, which is being revealed. The Hebrews of those days and also today (2024) find it difficult to believe that God abolished the order of Aaron and raised up a Melchizedek priesthood according to the order of Jesus. That is, the priesthood that was exclusive of anyone not born of Levi was now changed to be the priesthood of Jesus' tribe, according to the order of Melchizedek, according to the tribe of Judah.

Hebrews 7:11-Another-Different Priest

If **indeed maturing** were **through** the Levitical **priesthood,** (**because upon** it the people **were-legislated**) what further need was there that **another-different Priest** should rise **according** to the **order of Melchizedek,** and not be **said according** to the order of Aaron?

1. Priesthood in Hebrew 7:11 is defined as "**priest-togetherness"** (hieros (priest) and sun (together, with).
    a. That is, we are "priests" "together" "with" our High-Priest, Jesus Christ!
2. If the Levitical priests-togetherness was instituted to bring some level of maturity; how much more maturity by the better hope of Jesus' Melchizedek priest-togetherness (**Heb 7:19).**
    3. Since the Levitical priest-togetherness administer legislation to the people, how much more legislation

by the Melchizedek priest-togetherness. The Lord Jesus ratified legislations. He is the Lawgiver **(Mat 5:21-48).**

4. "Maturity" in this verse is in context to legislating tithing **(Heb 7:8-11).**
   a. Tithing is a mature act that shows a facet of adulthood.
   b. Levitical priests were commanded to take tithe of the people, their brothers.
   c. The people are commanded to tithe to their brothers.
      i. The people are to tithe to the "priest-worker" even if the minister works **(1 Cor 9:1-14, Phil 4:15-19)**
      ii. Paul, through grace was a "minister," a **"'priest-worker' of the gospel of God"** **(Rom 15:15-16).**
      iii. Those being taught are to share all good things to the one who teaches you catechize/catechism-learning by Q&A) **(Gal 6:6).**
5. The law was translated (transferred) because the priest-togetherness was translated (transferred)
   a. Translation of the law means to "change-place" of the law relative to the priesthood and its participant (not abolishment of **all** laws) **(Mat 5:17)**
   b. Creative laws are **not** changed or abolished.
      i. For example, the Law that states "**Love** the Lord our God with all our hearts, soul, mind, strength" never changes.
         1. Idolators (those who don't love God) **hate** God **(Ex 20:5 w/Ex 20:3-5)**
      ii. The Law of loving your neighbor as yourself never changes.
         1. For example, do not hate/murder/commit adultery, etcetera.

      iii. The creative law of marriage between a male and female never changes (**Matt 19:4**).

         1. **Let no human change this law of marriage (Matt 19:6).**

  c. Some Redemptive laws are changed.

      i. There is to be no more animal sacrifices **(Heb 10)**.

      ii. All meats can be eaten with prayer, thanksgiving, and sanctification by the word of God (**1 Tim 4:3**)

      iii. Some may choose not to eat meat; however, this choice should be personal and should **not** become a doctrine (**Rom 14 w/1 Tim 4:1-3**).

      iv. Observing certain days, years and months are no longer mandatory (**Gal 4, Col 2**).

         1. **Note:** instituting dogmatic "dos and don'ts" is considered "religion of angels," "serving gods that are no gods," worldly elements, doctrines of men, etcetera (**Col 2:15-23 2, Gal 4:8-18**).

6. "Translation of the law" means that the priest-togetherness is now translated to be as follows:

  a. The administering of God's **"spiritual law"** being transferred from the order of Aaron to the Melchizedek order (**Heb 7:14-15 w/Rom 7:14**)

  b. The administering of the law being transferred from the tribe of Levi to the tribe of the Lord Jesus, the tribe of Judah (all believers in Christ) (**Heb 7:14-15, Rom 2:28-29**).

  c. The Law and priesthood are transferred from preaching the letter of the law that condemns preaching, through the eternal Spirit, which produces-life (**2 Cor 3**).

  d. The written Law is transferred from the law being written on stones to the Law being written in our hearts (**Heb 8:10-13, Rom 2:13-16, 2 Cor 2**).

7. The Melchizedek priest-togetherness is not according to the law based on fleshly genealogy for a person to become a priest.
   a. The Lord's tribe is Judah, not Aaron's tribe of Levi.
      i. Jesus' "Spirit" empowered life and indestructible eternal life supersedes Levi's fleshly weakness, being subjected to death (**Heb 7:23-24, Rom 8:1-3).**
   b. Melchizedek order becomes priest according to the **power of endless life (lit., power of an indestructible life) of the Lord Jesus (Heb 7:16).**
   c. Melchizedek priesthood is not according to the law of flesh genealogy, but priesthood according to the law of "power" of "indestructible" life-**Heb 7:16-22**
      i. Jesus is made the High Priest according to the power of an un-loosed (un-destroyed) life.
      ii. Jesus lives into the age (the eternal age)
      iii. Jesus lives into the age (the holy of holies)
      iv. Jesus was "carried-through" into the Second (behind the second veil in the heavens)
      v. Jesus lives into the age (the heavens)
      vi. Jesus lives into the age (the millennium age)
         1. The millennium age is the age after the first resurrection of the resurrected king-priests saints.
8. The phrase "according to" is from the Greek word "kata" which means down from (i.e., from a higher to a lower plane with special reference to terminus (end point) (J. Thayer)
   a. The Melchizedek ministry comes down from a higher place (the place of the Highest God) to bring things pertaining to God in the lower plane (the earth)

9. The word "order" is translated from the Greek word "taxis;" and it means to arrange (a military term), "an ordered troop" arranged in descending ranks.

    a. The order of Melchizedek involves warring against enemies **(Psalm 110, Gen 14:18-21, Heb 10:12-23, etc.)**.

        i. Judah, via David, and His Lord (Jesus), who is also David's greatest Son, prevailed according to the Melchizedek order against our enemies **(Matt 22:41-46 w/Psalm 110, Eph 2:6, Luke 10:17-19)**.

    b. The "order" of Melchizedek priesthood functions in their "portion" of offering the "incense" of prayer **(Luke 1:8-9, Heb 5:6-7, Ps 141:2, Rev 5:8, Rev 8)**

    c. The Melchizedek priestly "order" of functioning in the gifts of the Holy Spirit, especially relative to prophecy, speaking in tongues, interpretation of tongues, and so on **(1 Cor 14:40 w/1 Cor 14)**.

    d. Melchizedek priesthood "order" relates to steadfastness of faith **(Col 2:5)**

        i. In the Melchizedek priesthood, we walk by faith and not by sight **(2 Cor 5:7, Heb 11:5-6)**

            1. Walking by faith involves hearing the Holy Spirit, hearing God's preachers **(Rom 10:17 2/Rom 10:14-17, Heb 5:1, Rev 2:7)**.

10. The Melchizedek is "another-different" priest "order."

    a. The expression "another-different" is translated from the Greek word "heteros" which means "another-different kind" **and not** "another-same kind" like the Greek word "allos."

        i. The Lord Jesus' priesthood is **not** the **"same"** as Aarron' priesthood.

ii. The Lord Jesus' priesthood is "another" (Judah's) and it is a "different" order (no longer Levi's), but according to Melchizedek's.

iii. For example, the Aaronic priesthood administering the blood of animals could not mature the conscience. Jesus' "different" Melchizedek order, administering Jesus better blood, can mature the conscience of those who have faith in Jesus' blood.

b. Order of Melchizedek used six (6) or seven (7) times in scriptures depending on which Greek text is used.

i. The references of the order of Melchizedek are **Psalms 110:4, Heb 5:6, Heb 5:10, Heb 6:20, Heb 7:11, Heb 7:17, Heb 7:21 (see additional details under Hebrews 5:6 or Hebrews 6:20 in this text)**

Hebrews 7:12-Transference of the Priesthood
Because, the **priesthood** being **'translated,'** there **is-becoming** of **necessity,** a **translation** also of the law.

1. Priesthood that is cited in **Hebrews 7:12** above is better translated as "priest-togetherness."

a. The word "priesthood" is literally a Greek compound word meaning "priest togetherness"— (hieros (priest) and sun (together, with).

b. That is, we are Melchizedek priests together with our High-Priest, Jesus Christ!

2. The word translated means to change place, to transfer, to relocate, and so on **(For example, Adam, Enoch, and Elijah experienced translation (Gen 5:24 w/Heb 11:5, Gen 2:15, 2 Kings 2:1-10).**

a. Adam was translated between the earth and the third heaven, Paradise (the Garden of Eden).

  b. Enoch was translated "to" faith and "with" faith to not see death.
  c. Elijah was translated to heaven.

3. The priesthood being "translated" can mean the following:
  a. The priest-togetherness (priesthood) has "change-place" (transferred) from being "together" with the order of Aaron being "together" with the order of Melchizedek.
  b. The priest-togetherness (priesthood) has "changed-place" (transferred) from the tribe of Levi to the tribe of the Lord Jesus, the tribe of Judah.
  c. The priest-togetherness (priesthood) has "changed-place" (transferred) which means that becoming a priest of God is no longer according to the law based on fleshly genealogy.
    i. The law related to the Melchizedek is now based on Jesus' endless life, not fleshly genealogy.
    ii. That is, people who are called "ethnic" or indigenous birth or indigenous genealogy are not qualified or disqualified due to their genealogy according to the flesh (**1 Cor 1:25-31, 2 Cor 5:16-18, 1 Tim 1:3-7)**
    iii. The eternal Spirit qualifies Gentiles through faith in the Lord Jesus Christ **(Rom 15:15-16).**
    iv. Jewish priestly genealogy does not qualify or disqualify a person from being a part of the Melchizedek order. The great apostle Barnabas was a Levite **(Acts 4:36, see also 1 Cor 12:13).**
    v. Like the Gentiles, it is the eternal Spirit qualifies Jews through faith in the Lord Jesus Christ **(Acts 11:15-18, Rom 3:9-25).**

vi. We become kingly-priests through faith in Jesus, the Living Stone **(1 Pet 2:4-10).**

4. The translation of the priest-togetherness necessitates translation of the law.

    a. The law that was related to priesthood function is now translated (transferred) from Aaron's order (Levi) to the Melchizedek's order (the Lord Jesus').

       i. For example, there is a translation from the law of attaining forgiveness by works [that causes boasting against God) to "the law of faith" (justification by the faith in the Lord Jesus' sacrifices and faith in the blood of Jesus (**Rom 3:27 w/Rom 3:21-31 w/Heb 7:14**)]

    b. All legislation related to God's priesthood is now through our Lawgiver, Jesus, according to the Melchizedek Order (**Matt 5 thru Matt 7, Gen 49:10, Isaiah 33:22, James 4:12).**

       i. For example, Old Covenant legislation says, "you shall not commit adultery" (external emphasis, which still holds true)-**Mat 5:27**

       ii. Jesus' Melchizedek New Covenant legislation says, "whoever looks at a woman to lust after her already committed adultery with her **in his heart**" (emphasis on internal purity, in addition to the external requirement)-**Mat 5:28.**

       iii. The Old Covenant (the Law) could not give life; however, the Melchizedek gives life, eternal **(Gal 3:21).**

Hebrews 7:13-14-Melchizedek's Tribe, Judah

[13]Because, he of whom these things are spoken is **'of-another-different'** tribe **'partaking,'** from whom no **man towards-hold'** at the **Altar.** [14]Because, **'it-is-before-clear'** that

our **Lord rose out of Judah; into** which tribe Moses **spoke nothing about priesthood.**

1. The Lord Jesus is from "another-different" tribe, Judah. Thus, Jesus' High priesthood relates to another-different priest, Melchizedek.
2. The tribe of Judah along with the tribe of Joseph is elevated above the tribe of Reuben to have the "command" and "the birthright."
   a. The tribe of Judah is elevated above the tribe of Reuben to be the "Commander" (one who stands in front)-**1 Chron 5:1-2 w/Rev 7:5 w/1 Chron 4:1, Strong's #5057, #5046**
      i. Reuben lost his "command" because he defiled his father's bed (**1 Chron 5:1-2**)
         1. **Note:** Reuben points to those who can lose their "command" for defiling the heavenly Father's bed, which prophetically speaks of men who are sexually abusing the Lamb's wife (Jesus' Church members)
   b. The tribe of Joseph (spiritual and natural Josephs) was elevated above the tribe of Reuben to inherit the birthright **(1 Chron 5:1-2, Eze 47:13, Rev 7:6-8).**
   c. The Lord Jesus and His spiritual tribe of Judah (consisting of Jews and Gentiles, in Christ), also called the "Church of the **firstborns (plural),"** now have the "birthright," the "command," and all the blessings of the double portions (**Heb 12:23, Col 1:15, Rom 8:28, Col 1:18, Mat 1:25**).
3. The Melchizedek tribe of Judah now partakes and commands the ministry of the **altar** in place of Levi.

a. Altar by definition means a "sacrifice-place." The Lord Jesus (of the tribe of Judah) is our **Altar (Heb 13:10-16).**

    i. Therefore, since the "Altar" (the sacrifice-place) is now personified in the Lord Jesus, we partake of the Altar in Spirit, through faith.

4. Moses spoke **"nothing"** of Judah related to the altar.

a. Jesus' Melchizedek order of the tribe of Judah was kept a secret in the heart of the heavenly Father until God's appointed time **(Eph 3:1-5; 8-11, Heb 1-Heb 13).**

b. Jesus' Melchizedek ministry of Judah is part of the mystery of Christ that was **hidden** from generations and ages. It was even hidden from Moses **(Eph 3:8-11, Col 1:26).**

c. The Lord Jesus' Melchizedek ministry according to the tribe of Judah is part of the hidden and mature wisdom of God **(1 Cor 2:6-16, Col 2:2-4).**

d. Melchizedek's principles of God's priesthood according to the tribe of Judah are the hidden wisdom, only revealed through the Holy Spirit, **for the mature to practice (1 Cor 2:6-7 w/1 Cor 2:10-16).**

e. The principles of the Melchizedek order according to Jesus' tribe of Judah (His disciples) are part of God's hidden wisdom to be **spoken** to the "mature" saints **(1 Cor 2:6 w/Heb 5:11-15, Heb 7:4).**

f. Wisdom for the **"mature"** related to Melchizedek and the tribe of Judah is God's wisdom for the **"spiritual" (those who received the Holy Spirit)**-1 Cor 2:11-12, 1 Cor 2:6-7 w/1 Cor 3:1 w/1 Cor 2:10-16, 1 Cor 14:37.

g. Jesus' Melchizedek ministry is part of the hidden wisdom God reveals to the mature, expecting them to be conformed to the maturity of Jesus' Melchizedek order under the Lion of the tribe of Judah (**1 Cor 2:6-7, Rom 8:26, 1 Pet 2:9, Rev 5:5 w/Rev 5:1-10**).

    i. **Note:** When the **Lion of the tribe Judah** was revealed in **Revelation 5,** it was also acknowledged that those redeemed by the blood of the Lamb of God, out of every tribe, tongue, people and ethnics, are now "kings and priests"

5. **The Lord Jesus rose out of Judah**. Yes, King Jesus, the greater Judah who is our High Priest according to the order of Melchizedek came from the tribe of Judah (**Gen 49:8-12, Heb 7:13-14**).

    a. Judah is defined as to praised, to worship, to celebrate, to use the hand, to worship with extended hand.

    b. Judah is the Lord Jesus, the High Priest and all His spiritual tribe, "of-Judah" consisting of both Jews and Gentiles, or Judah and the tribe of Judah are also understood as the Lord Jesus and all His <u>spiritually circumcised</u> saints.

        i. Per Rom **2:28-29,** a "Jew," which literally means "of Judah," is a believer who is **"circumcised in heart"** "with-Spirit" and "to-spirit." All of Jesus' disciples are spiritual Jews. Hence, the Lord Jesus' tribe of Judah are circumcised in spirit to now administer at His altar as His royal priests.

        ii. (**Note:** in the Greek text, "spirit," in **Rom 2:29,** is "dative case," which means that the phrase "in spirit" is both "locative" and "instrumental." The **Holy Spirit** is the "instrument" by which the circumcision occurs "in" our hearts; and **our spirit** is the "location" where circumcision "in" the heart takes place. This circumcision occurs with the "finger of God," without human hands involvement **(compare Col 2:11).**

1. "Circumcision" signifies the Spirit of God "cutting" from the heart, of believers, their previous inability to "keep [God's] law" **(Rom 2:25-27).**

2. That is, **uncircumcision** in heart is the inability for a person to "keep God's law;" the law being summed up as loving God with all our hearts, minds and souls and loving one's neighbor as we love ourselves. **This truth of loving God and loving our neighbors is also a summary of the Melchizedek's order "more excellent ministry" of mercy, grace, truth, etc. (Rom 2:25-27 w/Matt 22:37-40, Heb 8:6).**

3. **Note:** An uncircumcised heart also resists the Holy Spirit **(Acts 7:5).**

c. Judah represents King Jesus whom His brothers in the Church shall praise and bow down to in the Melchizedek order **(Gen 49:8, Rev 5, Rev 7, Heb 2:12).**

d. Judah represents the Lord Jesus and His Melchizedek order who shall put their hands in the neck of all enemies by defeating the enemies through praise and worship to God **(Gen 49:8, 1 Cor 15:25, Psalm 8:2).**

e. Judah represents three-fold principles of the Lord Jesus and His royal priests as the prevailing Lion of Judah **(Rev 5:5).**

i. The first principle of the lion is the young lion as energetic **(Gen 49:9).**

1. For example, God's "energy" to energizing the Lord Jesus to conquer "Book-Town" (the Word of God)—**Joshua 15:15 w/Rev 5:5.**

> a. We are to also prevail in the Word of God as lions of God, in Christ, the Lion of Judah (**1 Cor 2, 2 Tim 2:15, Acts 6:4, Joshua 15:15**).
>
> 2. Jesus' prevailing Spirit enabling "worthiness" to open the seals of the book in the hand of Him who sits in the Throne (**Joshua 15:15 w/Rev 5:5**).

ii. The second principle is the mature Lion, the strongest (**Gen 49:9, Proverbs 30:30**).

> 1. For example, God, the Strongest, and His unlimited force used to eternally raise Jesus from the dead (**Eph 1:17-23**).
>
> 2. God's strength to bring to pass His prophetic sayings related to the mystery of Jesus Christ, and so on (**Amos 3:6-8, Rev 10:5-7, Mat 12:29, Rev 20:1-3, Phil 3:20-21**).

iii. The third principle is the mature female lion, the skilled huntress (**Gen 49:9**)

> 1. For example, the Lord Jesus and His Melchizedek order (priesthood of God's sons and daughters) engaging and destroying our enemies (**Gen 3:14-15, Eph 6:10-18,1 Cor 15:25, Heb 10:13, Rev 11:5()**).

f. Judah is representative of King Jesus and His Melchizedek priesthood utilizing "the Scepter" of Righteousness (scepter of immediacy, or well-placed scepter)-**Gen 49:10, Heb 1:8, Luke 3:4-5**

g. Judah represents the Lord Jesus, the Lawgiver of the Melchizedek's order (**Gen 49:10, Mat 5, etc.**)

h. Judah is representative of Shiloh (He who gives us safety and security).

i. This safety and security is in Jesus' Sabbath Rest and safety, realized, through faith in Him (**Heb 4:1-11**).

i. Judah is representative of the Lord Jesus to whom all people "obeys" and gathers (**Gal 49:10, Gal 3, Rom 15:12, etc.**).

j. Judah is also represented by a donkey and the foal (son) of a donkey, which was fulfilled in the Lord Jesus riding on the donkey and the colt of a donkey, as He entered Jerusalem, before His crucifixion, to the cry of the multitude, saying: "hosanna" ("save now!")-**Gen 49:11, Matt 21:2-7, Zach 9:9.**

k. Judah is the Lord Jesus whose own blood (shed by others) were spilled on His garments (**Gen 49:11, Rev 19:11-16**).

l. Judah is the Lord Jesus (Melchizedek) who sees through eyes washed with His "atonement" blood-**Gen 49:11**

m. Judah is representative of the Lord Jesus whose "teeth" [symbolic of His Melchizedek Body of believers above, in heaven (upper teeth), and His Body of believer below, in earth (lower teeth)] in their "order" (keeping their rank and place like our teeth), who are also "washed with milk" (washed "white" (pure) in God's "logical" Word concerning God's Grace)-**Gen 49:12, Eph 3:14-15.**

i. **Note:** the upper teeth and lower teeth in our mouth represents God's "washed" and "shorn" "sheep" in heaven and on earth (**Gen 49:12 w/SS 4:2, John 10, Eph 3:14-15, Eph 1:10**).

Hebrews 7:15-16-Jesus' Indestructible Life

[15]And **it-is** still **'more-abundantly'** if according to the **'resemblance'** of Melchizedek there arises **'another-different'** priest. [16]Who is **become** not after the law of a **fleshly** commandment, but after the power of an **un-down-loosed** life.

1. Jesus' Melchizedek order is not "another of the same kind" (allos) as the priesthood of Levi. It is "another of a different kind" (heteros)
   a. It is not exactly similar to Aaron's order of becoming a priest.
   b. The Melchizedek's order is "different" relative to qualification to be priest.
      i. The qualification to become part of the Melchizedek order of priesthood is now based on Jesus' endless life, not fleshly genealogy as the Aaronic priesthood.
      ii. Hers is the Apostle Peter's narrative on how to be a part of the Melchizedek priesthood, the royal (kingly) priesthood]
         1. You must believe, Jesus is the Chief Cornerstone-**2 Pet 2:6-7**
         2. You must be born again (born of God)-**1 Pet 2:3**
         3. You must come to Jesus seeing Him as resurrected-the Living Stone-**1 Pet 2:4**
      iii. Through faith in Jesus, we are now living stones; a built spiritual house-**1 Pet 2:5**
      iv. Through faith in Jesus, we are now a holy priesthood-**1 Pet 2:5**
      v. Through faith in Jesus, we are now a chosen generation (gene)-**1 Pet 2:9**

    vi. Through faith in Jesus, we are now a kingly priesthood-**1 Pet 2:9**

    vii. Through faith in Jesus, we are now "the people of God"-**1 Pet 2:10**

    viii. Through faith in Jesus, we now have God's mercy-**1 Pet 2:10**

2. The so-called inferior genealogy, propagated by some, does **not** disqualify you from the Melchizedek priesthood (**1 Cor 1:26-31).**

    a. All of God's royal priesthood are "regened" through faith in Jesus Christ and the Holy Spirit-**Titus 3:5**

      i. All believers are God's "holy nation" ("holy 'gene'")-**1 Pet 2:9**

      ii. God does not "call ... many nobles (lit., "well-gene")-**1 Cor 1:26-31**

      iii. "God has also chosen ... the "'ignoble'" ("without-gene")-**1 Cor 1:26-31**

    b. The Lord Jesus having "stood up" (resurrected) and by fulfilling the **Urim (His "Lights")** and **Thummim (His "Completions"),** He has "enrolled" from all peoples, those who accept Jesus, "who were not a people of God," into His royal priesthood (**Ezra 2:61-63 w/1 Pet 2:9-10).**

      i. **Urim** means lights and is representative of the Lord Jesus and Jesus' Lights.

        1. For example, the Jesus' gives illuminations by the Spirit of Wisdom and Revelation in the knowledge of Him (**Eph 1:17, Eph 2, Eph 3, Col 1).**

        2. The Lord Jesus is the Light of the world (**John 8:12).**

        3. The Lord Jesus's "Life" is the "Light of men" (**John 1:4)**

4. The Lord Jesus is the "true Light" (**John 1:9**)
5. The Lamb of God, Jesus, is the Light of New Jerusalem (**Rev 21:23**)
6. The Lord Jesus is the Light of the gospel (the gospel brings light)-**2 Tim 1:10**)
7. The Lord Jesus is the light (illumination of God) to the people and the Gentiles (**Acts 26:23**)

ii. **Thummim** is defined as completions, which represents all things Jesus completed.
1. The Lord Jesus' "fulfilled all things" in the scriptures to be "completed" by Him, excluding what was left behind for apostles-**John 19:28 w/Col 1:24**
   a. Jesus completed the drinking sour/bitter wine-**John 19:30**
   b. Jesus completed the crucifixion and the piercing of his hands and feet-**Psalm 22:16, John 20:20,25,27**
   c. The scriptures were completed that His killers parted the garments of Jesus and cast lots for His coat-**Ps 22:18; John 19:23-24, Luke 23:34**
   d. As the Brass Altar for sacrifices was covered in **purple** when in travel, so the Lord Jesus was covered **in purple** in his travel to be crucified completing the prophetic word about Himself-**Mark 15:20, Num 4:13**
   e. It was completed that His disciples would scatter from Him-**Zac 13:7, Mat 26:56**

f. It was completed that the Lord Jesus was numbered with the transgressors-**Mark 15:28, Isaiah 53:12**

g. It was completed that the Spirit of the Lord would anoint Jesus, the Christ-**Luke 4:12-21, Isaiah 61:1-1**

h. It was completed that none of Jesus' bones were broken-**John 19:36, Ps 34:20, Ex 12:46**

3. In the Melchizedek order prescribed according to endless life and not according to fleshy gene does **not** disqualify Aaronic priest or a natural Jew because of his genealogy.

a. Paul, a Benjamite Jew, is a "priest-worker" of the gospel according to the order of Melchizedek priesthood-**Rom 15:16**

b. There is always a remnant ("first fruit") of believing Jews according to the election of grace-**Rom 11:1-5, Rev 7:1-8, James 1:18, etc.**

MELCHIZEDEK, JESUS THE ETERNAL PRIEST

Interpretation-The Only Lasting High-Priest
The high priests according to the order of Aaron were not eternal high priests. They would die, like all humans, and remain dead. Thus, there were many high priests after Aaron (Eleazar, Eli, Zadok, Eliashib, Hilkiah, etc.). On the contrary, our Lord Jesus "remains" an eternal High Priest because, yes Jesus died; however, God raised Him from the dead and "carried" Him "trough" "into the age," "[glorified with God's] own self with the glory **He had with [God] before the world was**," living forever as the slain Lamb and High-Priest, according to the order of Melchizedek **(John 17:5, Rev 5:6)**. That is, our Lord Jesus' Melchizedek priesthood has always existed and functioned in eternity. Jesus is the eternal High-Priest, according to the order of Melchizedek, from eternity past (He was), eternity present (He is), and eternity future (he will always exist). Thus, we have "one" High-Priest, eternally, on our behalf for all who serves the living God, including those of the Jew and the Gentiles, including those of the Old Covenant and the New Covenant who are now made mature in conscience, through the sacrifice and the blood Jesus, the Christ.

Hebrews 7:17-Into the Age
Because he-is-witnessing, you are a **Priest into the age according** to the order of Melchizedek.

1. God, Himself, witnesses that the Lord Jesus is Priest according to the order of Melchizedek.
   a. The witness of God is greater than men's witness-**1 John 5:9, John 5:36**
2. The Lord Jesus is the High Priest into the age.

a. Jesus is the Melchizedek Priest into the age (the eternal age)

b. Jesus is the Melchizedek Priest into the age (the holy of holies)

c. Jesus is the Melchizedek Priest who was "carried-through" into the Second (behind the second veil in the heavens)

d. Jesus is the Melchizedek Priest into the age (the heavens)

e. Jesus is the Melchizedek Priest into the age (the millennium age)

   i. The millennium age is the age after the first resurrection, where saints rule with Christ as king-priests.

3. The phrase "according to" is from the Greek word "kata" which means down from (i.e., from a higher to a lower plane with special reference to terminus (end point) (J. Thayer)

   a. The Melchizedek ministry comes down from a higher place (the place of the Highest God) to bring things pertaining to God in the lower plane (the earth)

4. The word "order" is translated from the Greek word "taxis;" and it means to arrange (a military term), "an ordered troop" arranged in descending ranks.

   a. The order of Melchizedek involves warring against enemies **(Psalm 110, Gen 14:18-21, Heb 10:12-23, etc.)**.

      i. Judah, via David, and His Lord (Jesus), who is also David's greatest Son, prevailed according to the Melchizedek order against our enemies **(Matt 22:41-46 w/Psalm 110, Eph 2:6, Luke 10:17-19)**.

b. The "order" of Melchizedek priesthood functions in their "portion" of offering the "incense" of prayer (**Luke 1:8-9, Heb 5:6-7, Ps 141:2, Rev 5:8, Rev 8**)

c. The Melchizedek priestly "order" of functioning in the gifts of the Holy Spirit, especially relative to prophecy, speaking in tongues, interpretation of tongues, and so on (**1 Cor 14:40 w/1 Cor 14**).

d. Melchizedek priesthood "order" relates to steadfastness of faith (**Col 2:5**)

   i. In the Melchizedek priesthood, we walk by faith and not by sight (**2 Cor 5:7, Heb 11:5-6**)

      1. Walking by faith involves hearing the Holy Spirit, hearing God's preachers (**Rom 10:17 2/Rom 10:14-17, Heb 5:1, Rev 2:7**)1

5. The Melchizedek is "another-different" priest "order."

a. The expression "another-different" is translated from the Greek word "heteros" which means "another-different kind" **and not** "another-same kind" like the Greek word "allos."

   i. The Lord Jesus' priesthood is **not** the **"same"** as Aarron' priesthood.

   ii. The Lord Jesus' priesthood is "another" and it is a "different" order according to Melchizedek.

   iii. For example, the Aaronic priesthood administering the blood of animals could not mature the conscience. Jesus' "different" Melchizedek order, administering Jesus better blood, can mature the conscience of those who have faith in Jesus' blood.

b. Order of Melchizedek used six (6) or seven (7) times in scriptures depending on which Greek text is used. The references are **Psalms 110:4, Heb 5:6, Heb 5:10, Heb 6:20, Heb 7:11, Heb 7:17, Heb 7:21 (see**

> additional details under Hebrews 5:6 or Hebrews 6:20 in this text)

Hebrews 7:18-19-Eternal Maturity

[18]Because there is **indeed** an **'un-placing'** of the commandment **before-leading** for the **weakness** and **un-profitableness of-her**. [19]For the law made nothing **'mature,'** but the **'upon-into-leading'** of a **'better-government expectation'** did; **through** the which we **'near-squeeze'** to-**the** God.

1. The previous "commandment" that appointed priests based on fleshly genealogy was **weak** and **unprofitable**.
   a. Weakness means to be without-strength because of the sinful flesh nature-**Rom 8:3**
   b. Unprofitable is defined as not-heaped together, not-heaped up, not-accumulative, no-increase.
      i. Unprofitableness of the previous commandment was weak because of works without faith-**James 2:14, Gal 3:23-26**
      ii. Unprofitable of the commandment also due to the Law's inability to resurrector give life-**Gal 3:21**
   c. The previous commandment was weak and unprofitable because the Old Covenant redemptive laws could not bring anyone to maturity.
      i. The commandment/law could not mature the conscience (it could not remove the remembrance of sins that was atoned through animal's blood)-**Heb 10:1-2, Heb 9:9**
      ii. The commandment/law could not mature the spirits of just men-**Heb 12:23 w/Heb 11:40.**
      iii. The commandment/law could not mature faith-**Gal 3:13, Gal 3:3.**

      iv. The commandment/law could not bring any to mature salvation (contrast-**Heb 2:10 w/Heb 5:9**).

2. Better is defined dominion, mastery, government, better after dominating (i.e., controlling), stronger, more excellent.
   a. Thus, the Melchizedek priesthood is under a better government.
      i. We are under the better government of faith, hope, love, i.e., the dominion of the Holy Spirit and the love of Christ through faith-**Eph 3:14-20, 1 Cor 13**
      ii. We are no longer under the dominion of condemnation **(2 Cor 3)**.
      iii. Through Christ Jesus' grace to us, we are now under the dominion of God's Grace-**Rom 6:9**
3. Maturity is defined as reaching the end stage, think of a telescope extending one stage at a time to function in full length, think of television, telephone.
   a. The law cannot mature any believer because it is a fleshly endeavor-**Gal 5:3-10**
   b. The law functions on curses-**Gal 3:10**
      i. Jesus Christ has redeemed us from the curse of the law-**Gal 3:13-14**
   c. God's promises being fulfilled to us are not by law but through faith in Christ-**Gal 3:18 w/Gal 3:5-6**
4. God maturing us is governed by a better hope (expectation)
   a. Our Lord Jesus Christ is our Hope (Expectation)-**1 Tim 1:1**
   b. The Lord's saints are called in "one hope (expectation)"-**Eph 4:4**
      i. The expectation we shall be like Jesus when he appears (**1 John 3:2-3**).

ii. The expectation of incorruptible inheritance (great and eternal salvation) guarded in heaven (**1 Pet 1:3-5, Heb 2:3, Heb 5:9, I Thes 5:8**).

iii. The expectation of eternal life (**Titus 3:7, Titus 1:2**).

iv. The expectation of glory (Christ manifest "in" us in all facets of glory)-**Col 1:27, 1 Cor 2, John 2:11, John 11, 1 Cor 15, etc.**

5. Through this "one" and "better" hope (our Lord Jesus is our Hope), we draw near to the living God.

Hebrews 7:20-21-The Oath

[20]And inasmuch as not without an **oath** he became **Priest**: [21](**Yet** with the **oath through** him that said **towards** him, the Lord **swore** and will not **regret**, you are **'Priest**[11] **into the age.'**

1. The Lord Jesus was made the High Priest according to God's oath.

   a. God's oaths are immutable (**Heb 6:13 w/Heb 6:18**).

2. The phrase "the Lord ... will not repent," mean, "the Lord ... will not regret."

   a. The Lord God, the heavenly Father, has "no regrets" with regards to His Son Jesus, the Christ, being the High Priest forever (into the age) according to the **order** of Melchizedek.

   b. "Regret" is used six (6) times in the New Testament

      i. Six (6) is the number related to man (Adam was made on the sixth (6th) day)

      ii. God has no regrets towards those who accepts Jesus Christ as their Savior.

         1. The heavenly Father loves His believers as He loves Jesus **(John 17)**

---

[11] **Note**: This writing is according to the Alexandrian Texts (arguable considered to be the oldest text).

iii. God only regrets making mankind when "every imagination and thoughts of their hearts are evil 'all day'" **(Gen 6:5-8)**. Thus, God calls us to "repentance" [lit., change (the way we) think].

Hebrews 7:22-Eternal Better New Covenant
According to so much, Jesus **became Surety (lit., surety in-limb) 'of-better-government' Covenant.**

1. The word better is defined as dominion, mastery, government, better after dominating (i.e., controlling), stronger, more excellent.

2. The word covenant is defined according to the following:

   a. Strong's Concordance defines covenant, as cutting flesh into two (2) pieces and then walking between the pieces.

   b. This is seen in God's covenant with Abraham in **Genesis 15: 7-10, NAS:** [7]And He said to him, "I am the LORD who brought you out of Ur of the Chaldeans, to give you this land to possess it." [8]He said, "O Lord GOD, how may I know that I will possess it?" [9]So He said to him, "Bring Me a three-year old heifer, and a three year old female goat, and a three year old ram, and a turtledove, and a young pigeon." [10]Then he brought all these to Him and **cut them in two and** laid each half opposite the other; but he did not cut the birds .... [17]It came about when the sun had set, that it was very dark, and behold, there appeared **a smoking oven and a flaming torch** which **passed between these pieces.**

   c. Covenant is also seen in the crucifixion of Christ. Jesus Christ, was cut in the flesh (whipped, nailed, pierced with a spear, punctured with thorns). In addition, Jesus was placed between the **two** bad-actors, who were also nailed to crosses and their bones broken. Thus, Jesus' crucifixion **between** the two thieves is a picture of God's everlasting covenant with those who accept Jesus Christ as the Son of God, the Christ!

d. Covenant, through the lenses of Hebrew pictograph that also testify of Jesus, the Son of God, crucified.

    ii. The Hebrew word for **"covenant"** is **BRYTh (ברית) or brith.**

    iii. The first two letters of BRYTh are **BR (בר). "BaR"** is defined as "son," "heir," "wheat;" and as we discussed earlier, this is exemplified when Jesus addressed Peter as "Simon **Bar** Jonah," meaning Simon, **son** of Jonah.

    iv. In addition, whenever the Hebrew letter "yad" or "yud" (י) is used at the end of a word, "yud" can be translated as "my." Tav (ת) means mark, sign, cross, covenant. Thus, the Hebrew pictograph for "covenant" is my (God's)-son-crucified, or the cross (of) my-son. Yes, Jesus is the Covenant.

5. Surety is defined as guarantor, lit., guaranteeing with one's own limbs (our Lord Jesus' was crucified, whipped, pierced with spears and thorns in His limbs)

6. The New Covenant is eternal and cannot be abolished- **Heb 13:20**

Note: With all that said, one of the things related to Jesus' Melchizedek order is the truth that the heavenly Father "cut" the "eternal covenant" in the Spirit, in eternity, related to the redemption of mankind "before the foundation of the world," before He made Adam. In other words, the Melchizedek order was always the eternal priesthood prepared on behalf of mankind. The Aaronic order of priesthood was to be temporary until Christ came to implement in this world the eternal covenant-**Gal 3:24, Heb 13:20**

1. The Lord Jesus, the covenantal Lamb, and His redemptive blood, was "**foreordained before** the foundation of the world;" and He was **slain before** the foundation of the world-**1 Peter 1:19-20. Rev 13:8**
   a. This truth makes the sacrifice of Jesus, as the Lamb of God, an **eternal and redemptive High-Priest's function** in anticipation of the foundation of the world
   b. The references above shows the pre-placed covenantal redemptive work of God, the heavenly Father, according to the order of Melchizedek, in the Spirit of God, in the concealed, in eternity.
   c. For example, the scriptures make it very clear that "Adam 'passed over' the covenant" **(see Hosea 6:7 in BSB translation and the Septuagint (LXX) translation)**
   d. That is, as we learned earlier in this section, the Hebrew word for "covenant" depicts the Lord Jesus Christ, slain and crucified between two other crosses. Adam was aware of this eternal covenant that existed before he and his wife sinned! However, Adam chose to "pass over" Jesus' eternal covenant, and chose instead to hide from God's love-**Hosea 6:7 w/Gen 3:8-11 w/Heb 13:20 w/Rev 13:8**
   e. The **eternal covenant**[12] of the Lord Jesus' Melchizedek order is now established in the earth forever, as it was already established in eternity, through the resurrection of our Lord Jesus Christ-**Heb 13:20**

---

[12] Dr Samuel Soleyn calls the eternal covenant the "Master Agreement," or the "Master Covenant" that governs the Melchizedek order of priests

Hebrews 7:23-No Longer Many Priests
And they **indeed became** many priests, because they were **prevented** to **'beside-remain' through** death.

1. When the Aaronic priests died, they were not "carried-through" to heaven **(Gen 35:29; 49:29, Jos 2:10).**
   a. Thus, their respective duties as priest did not continue. the Lord Jesus, on the contrary, remains the only Hight Priest forever.
   b. In their death they were gathered unto their people and fathers in Abraham's bosom **(Gen 25:8; 35:29; 49:29, Jos 2:10, Luke 16:19-31).**
   c. **The Lord** Jesus now holds the keys of hell and death-**Rev 1:17-18, Rom 6:9**
   d. Hell, and death can no longer hold those who believe that Jesus is the Christ, the Son of God-**Rom 6:9, Phil 1:21-22**
   e. After Jesus' death, burial and resurrection, all believers now go to be with Christ in the heavens (into the age) after they fall asleep in Christ-**1 Cor 15:18, 1 Thes 4:14, Phili 1:23**

Hebrews 7:24-Jesus Remains Priest Forever
Yet, this man, because he **'remains into the age,'** has an **'un-transgressing' 'priest-togetherness.'**

1. The phrase He remains Priest "into the age," means that Jesus is the permanent High-priest.
   a. He "remains" High Priest eternally.
   b. He was "carried-through" into the heaven with His blood.
   c. Thus, the Melchizedek **priest-togetherness** also "beside-remains" permanently (in this life and in the heavens when we go to be with the Lord Jesus).
2. Jesus' priest-togetherness is un-transgressing.

a. The word "un-transgressing" is a compound word with the prefix "a" (without, not) and "para" (beside, near, against) and "baino" (to walk, to step), which means "not-change-base" (not changing your base from God's life); "not-change-walk" (not changing your walk with the Lord Jesus); and "not-change-step"(not substituting the steps of Christ Jesus for another)—**1 Pet 2:21, Rom 4:12, 2 Cor 12:18, 3 John 4, John 5:24**

b. Here are some references where (transgression) is used to give contrasts to the Lord Jesus being without transgression.

   a. **Matt 15:2-3**–It is used of transgressing God's command by traditions of men.

      1. This transgression causes one to be rooted up-**Mat 15:13**

   b. **Acts 1:25**–transgression Judas committed against Jesus.

      1. This transgression causes permanent destruction from apostleship.

c. Other priests were not permanent because of death **through** transgressions.

d. Other priests were not permanent because of death **caused by** transgressions.

e. Transgression can also be understood to mean walking from God's command to obey traditions of men.

f. Transgression is betraying the Lord to men of ungodly tradition (their traditions, not God's) for money.

g. Dying, in the context of **Hebrew 7:24,** is considered a result of "transgression."

h. Aaronic priests were not permanent because they did not remain into the age. Now, through Christ Jesus, when Jesus' disciples pass away, we go into the age where the Lord is to be with the Lord Jesus.

i. Jesus was resurrected permanently and beside-remains on our behalf "into the age."

j. We are permanent kingly priests—the "priest-togetherness" "with" the Lord Jesus Christ

k. Through Christ we are priests and kings together with the Lord in this life (**1 Pet 2:9**).

l. We "continue" as priests and kings "together" with Jesus Christ when we transition into the age to be with Christ (**Heb 7:23-24 w/1 John 3:2 w/Rev 5:10**).

m. Through our Lord Jesus, we continue live into the age in public with the Lord-**John 6:58, 2 Cor 5:6-9**

n. We will also be priests and kings together with Christ in the next millennium through the first the resurrection (**Rev 20:4-6**)

3. The word priesthood in this scripture reference (**Hebrews 7:24**) literally means "**priest-togetherness." It is the compound word** hieros (priest) and sun (together, with).

a. That is, we are permanent "priests" "together" "with" our Melchizedek High-Priest, Jesus Christ!

Hebrews 7:25-Eternal Intercession

Wherefore he is **able** also to **save** them **into** the 'all-finish' that come **to** God **through** him, **always living, interceding over** them.

1. The word save is referring to the salvation Jesus, our High Priest, offers through His redemptive work and His intercession on our behalf. There are three stages of salvation.

a. There is the common salvation, the salvation that comes through confessing the Lord Jesus and belief that God raised Jesus from the dead **(Jude 1:3, Rom 10:9-10)**

b. There is the great Salvation, the salvation for those who mature (all-extend) into manhood, and as a result of their maturity, they to rule the "world to come" with Christ **(Heb 2:1-10, Rev 20:1-6).**

   i. This "maturity" relates to be transformed to be like Christ Jesus in His love, faith, knowledge, etc.

c. There is the eternal salvation, the salvation for all saints that is forever **(Heb 5:9)**

2. The word "utmost" as translated in the King James Version is properly a compound word that means "all-finish," or "all-extend," or "all-complete," or "all-goal reached."

   i. This word, "all-finish," is also used in **Luke 13:11** with respect to a woman whom Jesus caused to be straightened out ("all-extend") after being bent over for 18 years by a spirit of weakness.

   ii. Therefore, in context of the Lord Jesus' intercession for us to "all-finish" relates to the Lord Jesus straightens us in spirit, soul, and body through His prayers over us.

3. The phrase "always living" simply means the Lord Jesus is always living to always interceding over us.

4. Interceding by definition means to obtain by hitting the mark. Therefore, the Lord Jesus through His constant intercession causes us to obtain His fully extended salvation (safety, deliverance, etc.)-**Rom 8:22-26, Rom 8:34**

Hebrews 7:26-The Fitting Eternal High-Priest
Because such **'High-Priest' 'fitting' to-us**, who is **intrinsically-right**, **not-evil**, **not-contaminated**, **space from** sinners, and **became higher of-the heavens.**

1. As previously defined in this book, High Priest means Chief Priest, First Priest, Ruling Priest, Beginning Priest, and Arch Priest.
   a. The Lord Jesus' is the High Priest according to the order of Melchizedek.
2. The phrase "became us" (KJV) is properly translated as to "tower up," "fitting."
   a. So, it is also written in **Hebrews 2:10:** "For it was **'fitting'** for whom are all things, and by whom are all things, in bringing many sons unto to glory to make the 'original-leader' of their salvation 'mature' through suffering.**"**
3. The word translated as holy in the reference above means to be "intrinsically-right" (Greek hosios). It is not the other typical word hagios used for holy.
   a. Therefore, Jesus' rightness is His nature. He is the "only" intrinsically Right-One (**Rev 15:4).**
   b. We were also given this intrinsically right nature because God recreated us as a "new man" in Christ (**Eph 4:24).**
4. The Lord Jesus' innocent reveals that Jesus had no-intrinsic-evil (no evil in His nature).
5. The Lord Jesus being undefiled means He was uncontaminated.
   a. Due to the eternal Spirit in the Lord Jesus, He was able to offer Himself **without spot** to God-**Heb 9:14**

b. **The Lord Jesus, Himself, made it clear that the "prince of this world" "has nothing in Me" (John 14:30).**
    i. The phrase "has nothing" literally reads "has no, not one thing,"
    ii. That is, the prince of this world did not have **"one thing"** in Jesus. The Lord Jesus is uncontaminated!
c. We were redeemed by the valuable blood of the Christ as a Lamb blameless and without spot (**1 Pet 1:18-19**).

6. The scripture reference also said that the Lord Jesus was separate from sinners. The phrase means to be "spaced" from sinners.
    a. The Lord Jesus was tempted at all points like us, yet without sin-**Heb 4:15**
    b. **Note:** when the Lord returns "out of the Second," "the Tabernacle which is called the Holy of Holies," His coming will be "spaced from sin" for His saints. In His coming, it will be **"salvation"** for His believers (**Heb 9:28 w/Heb 9:3, 1 Thes 5:9**).

7. The exalted Lord Jesus is Higher than the heavens.
    a. There is a place in God that is higher that the heavens!
    b. The exalted Jesus is highest in position of absolute ownership and authority to grant conquest-**Gen 14:19-20**
    c. Jesus is in God's right hand in the heavens far above all (the highest above) principalities, powers, authorities, world-governments, spiritual hurts in heavens, thrones, lords (**Eph 1:20-23**).

d. A principle of the "highest God" is that God is possessor of heaven and earth-**Gen 14:19-20**

e. Another principle of the "highest God" is that God delivers our enemies into our hand-**Gen 14:19-20**

f. The Lord Jesus ascended far above all heaven that he may fill all things (**Eph 4:8-10**).

    i. In His ascending on high (His Highness, His absolute authority) He captured captivity.

        1. The Lord Jesus "spear-captured" all of Satan's cohorts who previously captivated humanity. (**Col 2:15**).

g. Melchizedek ministry sees and understands that God is the Highest, above all (**Gen 14:20**).

h. Jesus being the Priest of the Highest is truth that torments demons to manifest (**Luke 8:28**).

i. God, the Highest, has dominion over demons, over Satan, over Satan's angels, over all creation now, in the millennium, and forever (**Rev 20:1-3, 1 Peter 3:22, Heb 1:13-14, 1 Cor 15:28**).

Hebrews 7:27-Jesus' One Offering Forever

Who need not daily, to 'necessitate,' as those **high-priest**, to offer up sacrifice, **'foremost over'** his own sins, and then **of-those of-the** people's; for this he did **once,** when he **'offered-up'** himself.

1. The Lord Jesus does not need to offer sacrifices daily for sins as the Aaronic order had to do (**Heb 10:1-4**).

2. The Lord Jesus only had to make "one" sacrifice for sins, "once" (**Heb 10:10-18**).

Hebrews 7:28-The Eternal Word of the Oath
Because, the law **'appoints'** men **'high-priest'** which have **'weaknesses;'** but the **Word** of the **oath,** which was **after** the law, Son, **'into the age, matured.'**

1. All the high priests before Jesus had weaknesses.
   a. They had the weakness of being subjected to death (**Heb 7:23**).
   b. They had the weakness of being subject to sins.
2. The Word of the oath with respect to the Lord Jesus has no weakness.
   a. Jesus was raised from the dead through the oath and lives forever according to the order of Melchizedek (**Heb 7:20-24**).
3. The oath makes the "Son," our Lord Jesus, the eternal High-Priest (**Heb 8:1, Heb 6:13-20, Heb 7:20-28**)
   a. Remember that Sonship also means being an heir of God (**Gal 4:6-7, Rom 8:14-17, Rev 21:7**).
4. Jesus our High Priest is matured "into the age."
   a. The Lord being matured into the age means He is matured into the eternal age.
   b. The Lord being matured into the age means that the Lord Jesus entered behind the veil in the heavens.
   c. The Lord being matured into the age means the Lord is King-Priest now as he will be the millennium age to come.
   d. The Lord being matured into the age means that the Lord is functioning as High Priest in the Holy places in the heavens.
   e. The Lord Jesus matured into the age means He is one with the heavenly Father, the highest heaven in the **"Great-togetherness."**

MELCHIZEDEK, THE GREAT-TOGETHERNESS

Interpretation-The Oneness

One of the difficult things to interpret about Jesus' High Priest Melchizedek order is Jesus' associated priests within the "Great-togetherness." In other words, in the interpretation of the difficult things of the Melchizedek order, it will be understood that there is eternal inclusion between Jesus in the right hand of God's "Great-togetherness," who is typified by Melchizedek, who was "carried-through" into the heavens; and there is the priesthood of Jesus' believers who are eternally "priests" "together" "with" the Lord Jesus, in this life and also when we transition to be with Christ. That is, as our Lord Jesus' priesthood is eternal "together" with God, the Father and "together" with God, the Holy Spirit, so are His royal priests a permanent priesthood "together" with our High-Priest, the Lord Jesus. We do not stop being priests "together" with Jesus after this life. We "continue" as priest when we enter "into the age," the same age our Lord Jesus currently resides in. Jesus remains a High Priest forever!

Hebrews 8:1-The Sum of the Great-togetherness

Now of the things which we have spoken this is the **'Head:'** We have such a **High-Priest**, who is **seated** in the right hand of the throne of the **'Great-togetherness'** in the heavens.

1. The word Sum (KJV) is defined as "Head." This is God's summation into the Head, Jesus, of all the order of Melchizedek principles outlined from **Hebrews 5** through **Hebrews 7** and now in **Hebrews 8** and so forth.
   a. All things in heaven and on earth are also summed up in Christ (**Eph 1:10**).

b. The Lord Jesus is the Head of every man (**1 Cor 11:3**).
c. The Lord Jesus is Head over all **"to"** the Church **(Eph 1:22)**.
d. Christ is the Head of the Church **(Eph 5:23)**.
e. Christ Jesus is the Head of the Body, the Church **(Col 1:18)**.
f. The Lord Jesus is the head of all principalities and authorities **(Col 2:19)**.
g. The Lord Jesus, the Living Stone, is the Head of the corner as the Highest foundation of His Church **(1 Pet 2:7)**.

2. High Priest in the context of **Hebrews 8:1** is the "summation" that Jesus is our High Priest according to the order of Melchizedek working in oneness of the "Great-togetherness" (the heavenly Father, the Son, the High Priest, and the Holy Spirits)—**John 17:5, John 17:20-26**

3. The Lord Jesus is seated in the right hand of God out of which His Hight Priest ministry functions from the seat or Throne of the "Great-Togetherness."

4. The Lord in God's right hand speaks of Jesus, our Melchizedek, is seated in the right hand of the right hand of God's Throne, ruling with the as King **(Rev 3:21)**.

5. "Majesty" wen defined in this line will give more clarity to my use of the phrase "Great-togetherness."

    a. Majety is translated from the Greek word "magalosune" (mega (great) and sun (together, with), hence the use of the phrase "Great-togetherness."

    b. "Great togetherness" is used three (3) times in the scriptures.

        i. Great-togetherness (megalosune) is used in **Hebrews 1:3** of the Lord Jesus seated in the right hand of the "Great-togetherness" upholding all things by the word of His power when He by Himself purged our sins.

    1. Jesus' living voice of His power is part of the "Great-togetherness" "with" the heavenly Father and the Holy Spirit that is upholding all things.

    2. Jesus' sacrifices and blood being part of the "Great-togetherness" with the heavenly Father and the Holy Spirit has purged our sins.

ii. Secondly, the "Great-togetherness" is also used in **Jude 1:25** in relation "with" the "only God as Savior."

    1. Salvation is by the "only God" in the "Great-togetherness" with the love of heavenly Father, the gift and communion of Holy Spirit, and the grace of the Lord Jesus. No other gods from any other religions around the world can save (**Acts 4:12, 2 Cor 13:14**).

    2. The "only God" is the God of our Lord Jesus Christ, the same God of the Church, the same God whom Israel according to the flesh say they serve. Jesus is also "the only begotten 'God'" [**John 1:18** (per the Alexandrian Text)]. Jesus is equal to God (**John 10:30, Phil 2:6**)

iii. Thirdly, Lord Jesus, the Melchizedek High-Priest, is seated in the right hand of the **Throne** of the "Great-togetherness. This, the oneness of the Father, the Son and the Holy Spirit working "together" seamlessly as the High Priest (**Heb 8:1**).

    a. The "Great-togetherness" of Christ (His blood); the eternal Spirit (His purity in Christ); and God, the Father (receiving the offering of Christ to Him on our behalf (**Heb 9:14**).

    b. The "Great-togetherness" of God's election of us, through the foreknowledge of God, the sanctification of the Spirit, and the sprinkling of the blood of Jesus **(1 Pet 1:2)**

    c. In the "Great-togetherness," there is Him who sits on the Throne (the heavenly Father, who is Love), there is the Lamb of God in the middle of the Throne (Jesus, the Lamb who takes away the sin of the world), and there is the Seven Spirits of God (seven horns and the seven eyes) on the Lamb of God and before the Throne as seven Lamps of fire, all working "together" in "greatness" **(Rev 4:2, Rev 5:6, Rev 4:5).**

6. The "Great-togetherness" also speaks of God's Melchizedek's Priest-togetherness in a variety of expressions related to "togetherness."

    a. "Great-togetherness" of the God's "priest-togetherness" is Jesus' disciples working "together" with the greatness of heavenly Father (His Love for us), the greatness of the Son, our High-Priest (His sacrifice for us), and the greatness of the Holy Spirit, our Comforter, and so on **(Heb 12:2, Heb 1:3, Rev 4:5).**

       i. For example, the greatness of the Lord Jesus' grace with us, God's love with us, the Holy Spirit partnership with us executing His priest work of salvation **(2 Cor 13:14)**

    b. God's Great-togetherness also consist of "righteous-togetherness." We are made "righteous" because of being "together" with our Melchizedek, "King of 'righteous-togetherness,'" the Lord Jesus Christ, through faith ministering God's mercy, grace, etc. **(Heb 7:2, Rom 3:21-26).**

c. God's "Great-togetherness" in "priest-togetherness" speaks of Saints being "together" with Jesus' Melchizedek's "priesthood." That is, we are only "priests" of God and Christ because of "togetherness" with Jesus, our High-Priest (**Heb 3:1, Heb 7:11, Heb 7:12, Heb 7:25, Rev 20:4-6, 1 Pet 2:9**).

d. The "Great-togetherness" as it relates to" holy-togetherness" means that we are only holy because of the Holy Spirit relationship with us and our reciprocal relationship with the Father, through the Lord Jesus.

    i. Holy-togetherness is the Greek word hagiosune, hagios (holy) and sun (together, with)-**Rom 1:4, 2 Cor 7:1, 1 Thes 3:13**

        1. Hagious (holy) originally means religious "awe," dreadful thing, venerate, worthy of veneration-**Strong's #40, #53**

        2. Hagios (holy) is also defined as different (unlike) others, distinguished, distinct (BibleHub.com)

        3. Hagiois (holy) means pure, holy, clean, un-adulterated, chaste, pure inside and out-**Strong's #40, #53**

   i. We are holy because of us being "together" with the Spirit of Holiness (**Rom 1:4**)

   ii. Holiness" is matured or completed through us being "together" with **"fearing"** the living God (**2 Cor 7:1**).

   iii. Holy-togetherness is being "together" with the Lord's "holiness" that fosters **"blamelessness"** before the God and Father of us, when the Lord Jesus comes (returns)-**1 Thes 3:13**

      e. We mature holiness "together" "with" the Spirit of Jesus (**2 Cor 7:1 w/Rom 1:4**)

7. Jesus our High Priest has been "carried-through" into the heavens.
   a. Therefore, His priesthood remains because He was "carried-through" "into the age" (heaven)-**Heb 7:24**
      i. Jesus' Melchizedek order presently functions both in heaven and on earth.
         1. Jesus is High Priest in the heavens (**Heb 8:1-2, Heb 9:24-28**).
         2. Jesus is High Priest on earth over the House of God (**Heb 3:1-6 w/Heb 10:21-25**).
8. The heavens are also defined as the Highest **(Heb 1:3)**.
   a. Per **Hebrews 1:3,** with **Hebrews 8:1,** the "heavens" (plural) is synonymous with the "highest."
   b. Highest means the highest in position of absolute ownership and authority to grant conquest (**Gen 14:19-20**).
   c. Jesus is in God's right in the heavens far above all (highest above) principalities, powers, authorities, world-governments, spiritual hurts in heavens, thrones, lords (**Eph 1:20-23**).
   d. A principle of the "highest God" is that God is the only possessor of heaven and earth **(Gen 14:19-20). God owns everything! God created** the heavens and the earth in the same duration **(Ex 20:11). Therefore, He owns them!**
   e. A principle of the "highest God" is that God delivers our enemies into our hand **(Gen 14:19-20).**

    i. The Lord Jesus ascended far above all heavens that he may fill all things (**Eph 4:8-10**).

    ii. In His ascending on high (which shows His absolute authority) He captured captivity (see previous explanation under **Hebrews 7:1**)

f. The Lord Jesus is Higher than the heavens (**Heb 7:26**).

    i. In the Lord position of the Highest, He is expecting His enemies to be made is footstool is by the authority of His highest position in God's right hand of power (**Heb 10:13, Heb 8:1, Heb 1:3, Gen 14:18-21, 1 Cor 15:24-28**).

g. Those who walk in the Melchizedek ministry sees God's "Great-togetherness" as the Highest authority (**Gen 14:20**).

h. The Lord Jesus being the Priest of the Highest is the truth of Jesus, "the Son" being the "Highest" which also torments demons to manifest-**Luke 8:28**

    i. Jesus, the Highest has dominion over all (as demonstrated in His dominion over demons/Satan's angels in the millennium)-**Rev 20:1-3, Rev 20:7-10**

    ii. Jesus bound Satan when he came the first time in flesh and Satan will be bound again in the abyss-**Mt 12:29 w/Mat 12:22-29 w/Rev 20:1-3, Rev 20:7-10**

        1. Satan's angels/demons are also judged and bound from the earth during the millennium.

Hebrews 8:2-Jesus, the Minister of the Holy Places

A **Minister** of the 'holies,' and of the **true tabernacle**, which the Lord **pitched,** and not man.

1. The "Minister" is Jesus, the "People-worker," for so the word minister is defined in the Greek. Jesus is our High Priest "working" on behalf His "people" (As an example of Jesus' priestly work, you may reference His high Priestly prayer on our behalf in **John 17**).
2. The word Holies (plural) represent both the Holy Place and the Holy Holies in the Tabernacle in the heavens- **Heb 8:1-2**
3. The Holies also represent the holy places of the consciences of believers **(Heb 9:11-13)**.
4. The true Tabernacle is the literal/spiritual Tabernacle in heaven, that Moses was admonished to copy exactly **(Heb 9:24, Heb 8:4-4, Rev 15:5)**.
5. The true Tabernacle is God's people as written in **Revelation 13:6** (see oldest Greek text, i.e., the Alexandrian)
6. The true Tabernacle is New Jerusalem, the New "Priest-Peace" **(Rev 21:3)**
   a. The Greek word for Jerusalem is "Hierousalem" a compound word consisting of hierou (priest, sacred, temple) and Salem (peace) (see Strong's 2419, BibleHub.com)
      i. Hence, New Jerusalem means New Priest-Peace
   b. This is the New **"Salem"** for Jesus' Melchizedek "priests" that was prefigured in **Genesis 14:18**
7. The word pitched means to fasten a tent, peg-fixed, build by fastening together.
   a. The Lord Jesus, Himself, built the true Tabernacle in heaven, just as Moses built the exact copy on earth.
   b. We are also the Lord's tabernacle being built without man's hands **(Dan 2:34; 2:45, Dan 5:5, Dan 8:25, Ezekiel 8:1-3, Col 2:11)**.

    i. A spiritual application of us being the Lord temple being built without human hands is exemplified in **Colossians 2:11**

Hebrews 8:3-Jesus' Offering

For every **'high-priest'** is **ordained** to offer both gifts and sacrifices, **therefore,** it is of **'constraint'** that this man has **something** also to offer.

1. High-priests are appointed in things **"towards"** God (**Heb 5:1 w/Heb 2:17**).
   a. "Things towards God" include "making propitiation for the sins of the people"-**Heb 2:17, Luke 18:13**
   b. "Propitiation" is translated from the Greek word hilaskomai which also means cheerful mercy, cheerful grace, atonement related to sins (**Luke 18:13, see Strong's #2433, #2434, #243**6)
   c. It is the Son whom God have committed all judgments to who decides our eternal punishment or our eternal life based on the atonement of sins or the lack thereof—**John 5:22.**
   d. The heavenly Father wants to atone (forgive) our sins; however, we must ask for His clemency. He also requires that we forgive others as he forgives us.
2. High-priests **offer to God** both gifts (plural) and sacrifices (plural)
   a. Offerings represent Jesus' prayers and supplications, and so on (**Heb 5:7**).
   b. Offerings represent Jesus who sacrifice Himself, and so on (**Heb 9:26, Heb 7:27, Eph 5:2**).
3. The word "necessary" means "constrained" and speaks to the Lord Jesus, according to the order of Melchizedek, who constrained Himself to offer gifts and sacrifices to permanently atone for our sins.

4. The phrase "this **Man** has something also to offer" speaks of the matured **"Man"** Jesus **(John 4:29)**
    a. "He offered one (first) sacrifice for sins "into the carried-through" into the heavens **(Heb 10:12).**
    b. The Lord Jesus being "carried-through," He is now seated in the right hand of God in the heavens **(Heb 10:12 w/Heb 8:1).**
    c. Jesus, our Melchizedek, is seated in the right hand of God, expecting until His enemies be made His footstool **(Heb 10:12 w/Heb 8:1).**
    d. The Lord Jesus, "'because' by one (first) offering, He has matured **'into the carried-through'** those (us) being sanctified" **(Heb 10:14)**
        i. Through the offering of Jesus, we are already "carried-through" and seated with Him upon the heavens **(Eph 2:5-7, Phil 3:20)**
            1. Thus, believers in Christ Jesus are part of the "Great-togetherness" in the heavens, "having therefore confidence brother 'into the entering the 'holy-places' in the blood of Jesus" **(Heb 10:19).**
            2. Enter holy-places where?
                a. Entering the "holy-places" of the true tabernacle in heaven where our Melchizedek, Jesus, is seated in the right hand of the "Great-togetherness"-**Heb 8:1-2, Eph 2:5-7**
                b. Enter holy-places in heaven how? We enter the holy places in the blood of Jesus **(Heb 10:19 w/Heb 12:24).**
                c. Enter the holy-places in heaven how? We enter by the "way" (hodos) of Jesus, the "'freshly-slain' sacrifice" **(Heb 10:20 w/Rev**

5:6, John 14:6). The shed blood of our Lord Jesus and the sacrifice of Himself is as "fresh" now as it was 2000 years ago.

5. **Note:** it is from the "holy-places" in the heavens, from the "true tabernacle," "in the right of God in the heavens," the Lord Jesus, the High Priest of the Highest and His royal priesthood (those who are "carried-through" and seated with Him upon-heavens) according to the order of Melchizedek (Jesus and His the twenty-four priests king elders) will continue to minister until the completion of this age; and they will continue to minister during the age to come (the 1000 year rule of the priests of God and Christ, after the first resurrection)-**Rev 20:4-6, 1 Cor 4:8, Heb 10:12-13, Heb 1:3, Psalm 110, Rev 4:1-2, Rev 4:4, Rev 15:5-8 w/Rev 21:9 w/Rev 22:8-9; Rev 17:1 w/Rev 19:10, etc.**

With all that was said concerning **Hebrews 8:3**, the "Great-togetherness" also consists of the Heavenly Father in His throne **(Heb 12:2);** the Son Jesus our High Priest in the right hand of the Throne **(Heb 8:1;** the Seven Lamps of the Seven Spirits of God before the Throne **(Rev 4:5, Isaiah 11:1-2)**; the kingly priesthood of the twenty-four elders (representative of the matures believers) around God's throne **(Rev 4:4);** those "saved by grace "seated together upon the heavens in Christ Jesus **(Eph 2:6, Heb 10:4);** all working together **as one** that the world may believe that the heavenly Father sent Jesus-**John 17:21**

Hebrews 8:4-Jesus's Offering upon Heaven

Because, if he were on earth, he should not be a priest, seeing there are priests that offer gifts **according to** the law.

1. The Phrase "if he were on earth, He should not be a priest" literally reads, "If indeed then he-was on earth not **'up'** he-be a priest."
   a. The Lord Jesus is the **"up"** High-Priest
      i. The Lord Jesus is the heavenly (up) High-Priest
      ii. The Lord Jesus is not a High Priest by earthly assignment.
2. The phrase, "if he were on earth," does not mean the Lord does not minister in the earth. It means he does not minister according to the Aaronic priesthood that superseded by the Melchizedek order.
   a. The Lord Jesus is now seated in the right hand of the Heavenly Father **(Heb 8:1);** who also traverse to the earth as our High Priest as needed **(see Acts 23:11, Acts 9:1-6, Acts 9:10-19)**
3. The phrase He "should not be priest" means the Lord Jesus' Priesthood is not according to priests that offer gifts, as animal sacrifices, according to the Law of the old covenant (**Heb 8:4**)
   a. These gifts of the priests on earth can never take away sins-**Heb 10:11**

Hebrews 8:5-The Patterns in Heaven

Who **serve** unto an example and a shadow of '**upon-heavens,**' as Moses was **warned** of God when **'impending'** to '**complete**' the tabernacle: for, **see**, **he says**, that you make all things according to the **'type'** showed to you in the mountain.

1. The tabernacle Moses built on earth, according to the **pattern ("type")** he saw were shadows of the heavenly things.

a. **Note**: the "patterns" of the tabernacle were always intended to be an example of heavenly things. It was not meant to be a permanent function in the earth **(Gal 3:13)**.

b. The thing Moses built are **"not the very image of the things"** God will implement in His saints **(Heb 10:1)**

   i. The Lord Jesus' sacrifice of Himself is **"the very image"** of God's intent to provide eternal redemption and eternal inheritance **(Heb 9:14-15-Heb 10)**.

   ii. The Boby of believers are the true temple of God; manmade buildings are **not** the temples of God)—**1 Cor 3:16 w/Acts 17:24**

   iii. The true temple of God is the Tabernacle in heaven, the Lord Jesus erected **(Heb 8:2 w/Rev 15:4-8)**.

2. The tabernacle Moses built is called a "worldly sanctuary" **(Heb 9:1)**.

a. This means that any so-called man-made church buildings on earth are considered worldly.

b. The "worldly sanctuaries" will be abolished and burned down **(Matt 24:1-2)**.

3. The Tabernacle Moses built was called a "type." Per the Greek origin of the word "type," a type is a model forged by striking something repeatedly, a copy, etc.

a. We being "forged" into the heavenly "type" is also accomplished through teachings **(Rom 6:17)**.

b. True apostles are "types" whom the saints are to imitate **(Eph 5:1-2, Phil 3:17, 2 Thes 3:9)**

c. Like the saints a Macedonia, Jesus' disciples are also types to be copied **(1 Thes 1:7)**.

   i. Therefore, living righteously matters to our fellow man who observes us **(Job 35:7-8)**.

JESUS' MELCHIZEDEK BETTER COVENANT

Interpretation-The New Covenant

The teaching of the Melchizedek order in the Book of Hebrews makes it clear that the Melchizedek order is the order of God's priesthood in the New Covenant; and it was always God's plan for Jesus' Melchizedek order to supersede the previous temporary priesthood under the first Covenant that was provisionally added until the Seed, Christ, came **(Gal 3:19-25)**. The New Covenant is called the "better" Covenant, "legislated upon better promises." This order of Melchizedek (Jesus, our High Priest, and His priests) is also called a "more excellent ministry" based on the better New Covenant **(Hebrew 8:6-13, Hebrews 10)**. With that said, before, I exegete some of the Greek words in the verses related to the section, I will list some of the "better things" of the Melchizedek order under the New Covenant.

Hebrews 8:6-More Excellent Ministry

But now has he **obtained** a **more excellent ministry,** by how much also he is the **mediator** of a **better covenant,** which was **established** upon **better promises**.

1. The word **"obtain"** is translated from the Greek word "tugchano;" and the word means to hit the mark, spot on, hit the bullseye, to reach, to get, obtain ["tugchano" is the opposite of "mamartano" (to miss the mark)]. This word is also used in the Greek word for intercession **(Heb 7:25)**. The Lord Jesus **obtained** a more excellent ministry!
2. More Excellent is derived from "diaphero," transliterated to English, word **"different."** Yes, in reading the book of Hebrews, the Four Gospels, it can easily be seen that the

Lord Jesus was **different** from the religious leaders of His day and sinful mankind in general.

    a. The more excellent ministry is a ministry with a "more excellent name," Son or sonship (**Heb 1:4-12**).

3. The word **"better"** is defined as dominion, mastery, government, better after dominating (i.e., controlling), stronger, more excellent.

4. Here are some of the better promises.

    a. We have "sonship" a better name than angels-**Heb 1:4 w/Gal 4**

    b. The blessings of Melchizedek's more excellent ministry are better than the curse of the Law-**Heb 7:7**

    c. There is a better hope of Jesus indestructible High Priesthood, the hope of resurrection-**Heb 7:19**

    d. Jesus's sacrifices are better (**Heb 9:23).** That is, the blood of Jesus purges us from the consciousness of sins, etc.

    e. Believer has better possessions in God-**Heb 10:34**

    f. Believers have a better heavenly "father-land"-**Heb 11:14-16**

    g. We have the opportunity for a better resurrection-**Heb 11:35, 1 Cor 15, etc.**

        i. Better resurrection is linked to those who belong to Christ; obtaining a better resurrection relates to the degree of suffering one endures/experience; better resurrection is linked to the type of "seed" that is sown by words in your hearts; better resurrection is also linked to the practices we do in our bodies-**Heb 11:35, 1 Cor 15:38, 1 Cor 15:23, 2 Cor 5:10, etc.**

    h. Through Jesus blood we have a better maturity in conscience-**Heb 11:40 w/Heb 10**

   i. We have a better maturity in eternal inheritance linked to our consciences being purged (this better inheritance is for the Old Covenant saints as well as the New Covenant saints)-**Heb 10:49 w/Heb 9:14-**15

   j. Jesus shed the better blood that speaks forgiveness and not revenge-**Heb 12:24**

5. The Mediator speaks of the Lord Jesus who is the only Mediator between God and man-**1 Timothy 2:5**

6. The better covenant can be understood by definition, contextual use, and Hebrew hieroglyphics.

   a. Strong's Concordance defines covenant, as cutting flesh into two (2) pieces and then walking between the pieces.

   b. This is seen contextually in God's covenant with Abraham in **Genesis 15: 7-10,** NAS: [7]And He said to him, "I am the LORD who brought you out of Ur of the Chaldeans, to give you this land to possess it." [8]He said, "O Lord GOD, how may I know that I will possess it?" [9]So He said to him, "Bring Me a three-year old heifer, and a three year old female goat, and a three year old ram, and a turtledove, and a young pigeon." [10]Then he brought all these to Him and **cut them in two and** laid each half opposite the other; but he did not cut the birds .... [17]It came about when the sun had set, that it was very dark, and behold, there appeared **a smoking oven and a flaming torch** which **passed between these pieces.**

   c. Covenant is also seen in the crucifixion of Christ. Jesus Christ, was cut in the flesh (whipped, nailed, pierced with a spear, punctured with thorns). In addition, Jesus was placed between the **two** bad-actors, who were also nailed to crosses and their bones broken. Thus, Jesus' crucifixion **between** the two thieves is a picture of God's everlasting covenant with those who accept Jesus Christ as the Son of God, the Christ!

    d. Covenant, through the lenses of Hebrew pictograph also testify of Jesus, the Son of God, crucified.

        i. The Hebrew word for **"covenant"** is **BRYTh (ברית) or brith.**

        ii. The first two letters of BRYTh are **BR (בר). "BaR"** is defined as "son," "heir," "wheat;" and as we discussed earlier, this is exemplified when Jesus addressed Peter as "Simon **Bar** Jonah," meaning Simon, **son** of Jonah.

        iii. In addition, whenever the Hebrew letter "yad" or "yud" (י) is used at the end of a word, "yud" can be translated as "my." Tav (ת) means mark, sign, cross, covenant. Thus, the Hebrew pictograph for "covenant" is my (God's)-son-crucified, or the cross (of) my-son. Yes, Jesus is the Covenant.

7. The word **"established"** is defined as **"legislated."**

    a. The Lord Jesus is the Law Giver-**Isaiah 33:22, James 4:12**

    b. The Lord Jesus gave new legislation according to the order of Melchizedek-**Matt 5 through Matt 5, Heb 7:11-12**

    c. The writers of the New Covenant books (Matthew, Mark, Luke, Apostle John, Apostle Peter, Apostle Paul, Apostle James, Jude, the Writer of the Book of Hebrews) "legislated" according to the order of Melchizedek.

8. Some of the better promises of the New Covenant are as follows:

    a. God does not remember our sins, once we are forgiven—**Heb 8:12**

   b. The Laws of God are written in our deep thought and heart—**Heb 8:10**
   c. We will know the Lord for ourselves because His Laws are "in" us—**Heb 8:11**
   d. God Himself will teach believers—**Heb 8:11**

Hebrews 8:7-Faulty Old Covenant

For if that **first covenant** had been faultless, then should no place have been **sought for the second.**

1. Fault was found in the First Covenant
    a. The Old Covenant laws were written on tables of stones and not tables of the heart-**Heb 8, 2 Cor 3**
    b. The Old Covenant laws could not purge the conscience-**Heb 9, Heb 10**
    c. The Old Covenant laws made a remembrance of sins every year with the yearly sacrifice. They could not forget their sins-**Heb 10**
    d. Sin used the law against humanity-**Rom 7**
2. The Second Covenant is the New Covenant
    a. The New Covenant is under the Melchizedek order relative to redemption, the eternal redemption—**Heb 9:12-15, Rom 8:23.**

Hebrews 8:8-A New Covenant

For finding fault with them, he says, behold, the days come, says the Lord, when I will make a **new covenant** with the **house of Israel** and with the **house of Judah:**

1. God found fault with **"them"** of the Old Covenant
    a. "Them" can represent those who came out of Egypt with Moses, etc.-**Heb 8:9**
2. God then made a New Covenant

a. This New Covenant is mediated by the Lord Jesus-**Heb 9:15**

b. The New Covenant is ratified by the better blood of Jesus-**Heb 10:29**

c. The New Covenant became "forceful" through the death, blood, and resurrection of the Lord Jesus-**Heb 9:17-18**

d. In the New Covenant, believers are given the Spirit of Grace, if they request to be filled with God's Spirit-**Luke 11:9-13, Heb 10:29, Acts 10**.

e. The New Covenant is based on "better promises."

   i. It is ratified by the better sacrifice and better blood of Jeus Christ as opposed to animal blood.

   ii. We can now be "matured" in conscience through Jesus' Melchizedek New Covenant, and so on.

3. The House of Israel

a. It is understood that the book of Hebrews was originally written to the Hebrews (all Israelites).

   i. However, it is also true that the Melchizedek priesthood, God's promises, and the teaching of the book of Hebrews is for any "man" (human) who are in Christ, God's sons of glory consisting of Jew and Gentiles **(Heb 2:9, 1 Pet 2)**

b. To the Israelites "first" pertains the "sonship," the glory, the covenants, the giving of the law, the service of God, and the promises-**Rom 9:4, Rom 1:16, Rom 2:10, Eph 2:12**

c. **Note**: the statement above does not mean that the Gentiles were an **"afterthought."** The Gentiles were also God's plan for "sonship" **before** the foundation of the world-**Eph 1, Eph 2, Eph 3, etc.**

d. The heavenly Father chose Israel to be the nation, through the tribe of Judah, who is to bring forth the

Promised Seed (Jesus, the Christ) of the Holy Spirit to be a blessing to both the Jews and Gentile through the blessing of Abraham-**Matt 1:18 w/Gal 3:7-9**

e. The Twelve Tribes of Israel were only **"some"** of God's First-fruits of believers-**James 1:18, Rev 7:1-8, Rev 14:1-5**

4. The House of Judah

a. The House of Judah hints to the mystery Christ of the Melchizedek order that was hidden in God and is now functioning through the House of Judah, the household, and the tribe of our Lord Jesus Christ-**Heb 7:11-15, Matt 1:1-17, Luke 3:23-38**

Hebrews 8:9-Not the Old Covenant

Not according to the covenant that I made with their fathers in the day when I took them by the hand to lead them out of the land of Egypt; because they continued not in my covenant, and I regarded them not, says the Lord.

1. The New Covenant will "not be according to the covenant God made" with natural Israel when he took them out of Egypt-**Ex 24:3-11, Ex 34:10, 27, 28.**

a. The Old Covenant is established by the blood of cows, goats-**Heb 9:19-22.**

2. The New Covenant will be according to the Melchizedek order-**Heb 8:10**

a. The New Covenant is established by the blood of Jesus-**Heb 9:14-18**

Hebrews 8:10-Hearts and Deep Thoughts

For this is the **covenant** that I will make with the house of Israel after those days, says the Lord; **I will put my laws into their mind,** and **write them in their hearts:** and I will be to them a God, and they shall be to me a people:

1. The New Covenant consists of God placing and writing his laws in the hearts and mind (deep thoughts) of the Israelites who accepts Jesus Christ-**Heb 8:10, Heb 10:14-18**
2. New Covenant consists of God writing the law in the hearts of the Gentile believers who accepts Jesus as the Christ-**Rom 2:15, 2 Cor 3:1-6**
3. New Covenant is also for the Gentile believers-**1 Cor 11:25, Eph 2:11-22**
   a. There is now no distinction between the believing Jews and the believing Gentiles-**Rom 10:12, Rom 3:22, Gal 3:28**
      i. Thus, priesthood relating to the Melchizedek is for both Jews and Gentiles.

Hebrews 8:11-The Least and the Greatest

And they shall **not teach** every man his neighbor, and every man his brother, saying, **know the Lord**: for all shall know me, from the **least** to the **greatest.**

1. In the New Covenant God, Himself, will make Himself known to his people.
2. In the New Covenant, there is equality of God making Himself known to both the least and the greatest saint.
3. Though God gives "teachers" to mature the Body of Christ, the heavenly Father is also personally involved in teaching us with respect to His mercy, discernment, and so on-**1 John 2:20-21, 1 John 2:27**
4. Knowing the Lord is knowing experientially His mercy.
5. Knowing the Lord is knowing experientially that God does not remember our unrighteousness, lawlessness, and sins once He forgives us-**Heb 8:12** (see following scripture).

Hebrews 8:12-God Remembers no More

For I will be merciful to their **unrighteousness,** and their **sins** and their **iniquities** will I **remember no more.**

1. The phrase "for I will be merciful" is referring to God Himself teaching His people to know Him personally that he is a merciful; and He is kind God-**Heb 8:11, Exodus 34:6**.
2. **Through the forgiveness** of the blood of Jesus, under the New Covenant of the Melchizedek order, the heavenly Father does not remember our unrighteousness, lawlessness, and sins.

Hebrews 8:13-Vanished Old Covenant

In that he says, A **new covenant,** he hath made the first **old.** Now that which **decays** and **waxes old** is ready to **vanish away.**

1. The New Covenant is in and through the better blood of Jesus and the Spirit of Grace-**Heb 10:29**
   a. The New Covenant is mediated by the Lord Jesus-**Heb 9:15**
   b. The New Covenant is ratified by the better blood of Jesus-**Heb 10:29**
   c. The New Covenant became "forceful" through the death, blood, and resurrection of the Lord Jesus-**Heb 9:17-18**
   d. In the New Covenant the heavenly Father gives the Spirit of Grace to believers-**Heb 10:29, Acts 10, Acts 19, Acts 2**
2. "Making the first old," "old" being the operative word in this point, means the first Covenant is now considered "ancient," and "senile."
3. The Old Covenant is decayed and became old.

4. The Old Covenant is "become old;" and it is now considered senile (weakness due to old age)
5. Two thousand years ago, during Jesus' days in the flesh, the Old Covenant was considered vanishing away. The Old Covenant is vanishing and shall disappear permanently.
   a. The Old Covenant is now obsolete-**Heb 10:9**
      i. The heavenly Father **violently took away** the first Covenant that he may establish the second covenant.
         1. The Lord Jesus' being **"taken away"** by the death of the cross was "violent"-**Strong's #337**
   b. If a person forsakes the New Covenant and turns back to the Old Covenant (of animal sacrifices), it is an insult to the Spirit of Grace. It is considered as trampling underfoot the Son of God and making the Lord Jesus's' blood of the New Covenant common-**Heb 10:29**

MELCHIZEDEK'S BREAD AND WINE

Interpretation-Abraham Receiving Communion

God's eternal plan to have a High Priest according to the order of Melchizedek, the order of the Lord Jesus Christ, was first revealed to Abraham when Melchizedek met Abraham long ago. And when Melchizedek was first introduced to Abraham, he brought forth bread and wine to Abraham and Abraham's men after the war with the various kings to free Abraham's nephew, Lot. Bread and wine are representative of communion table of the body of our Lord Jesus that was broken for us; and the blood the New Covenant in Jesus' "better blood." Hence, Melchizedek ministered the "Lord's Supper" to Abraham and his men. And Abraham, like New Covenant believers, partook of the broken body of Jesus (the bread), and blood of the New Covenant (the wine) that Melchizedek brought forth to Abraham.

The Lord's Supper to Abraham

1 Corinthians 11:20; 23-25: When you come together therefore into one place, this is not to eat the Lord's supper .... [23]For I have received of the Lord that which also I delivered unto you, that the Lord Jesus the same night in which he was betrayed took **bread:** [24]And when he had given thanks, he **broke it**, and said, take, eat: this is my **body, which is broken** for you: this do in remembrance of me. [25]After the same manner also he took the cup, when he had supped, saying, this cup is the **New Covenant** in **my blood:** this do you, as often as you **drink it,** in remembrance of me.

Genesis 14:18-19: [18]And Melchizedek king of Salem brought forth **bread and wine:** and he was the priest of the **Highest**

God. [19]And he blessed him, and said, Blessed be Abram of the **Highest God,** possessor of heaven and earth:

As the New Covenant saints partake of the bread and wine of the Lord's Supper, so Melchizedek ministered to Abraham the New Covenant in the broken body of the Lord Jesus, as the bread, and the New Covenant in Jesus' blood, as the wine. The New Covenant was ratified through the offered sacrifice of the body of our Lord Jesus and through the offered blood of our Lord Jesus. And with respect to both the offering of the sacrifice of the body of Jesus and the offering of the blood of Jesus, they were accomplished and witnessed through the "Eternal Spirit" **(I John 5:6, Heb 9:14).**

Abraham and Jesus' Wine

That is, in **2 Corinthians 3:17,** we learn that "the Lord is the Spirit;" therefore, it is the Spirit of the Lord Jesus who can both sprinkle the holy-places in heaven, so we can enter the holy places in the Spirit; and simultaneously it is the Spirit of the Lord Jesus who sprinkle our conscience, so we can serve the living God. It is the Holy Spirit who witness to us that God does not remember our sins once we accept His forgiveness through the sacrifice of the body of Jesus, the Christ **(see 1 John 5:8, Heb 10:14-18, Heb 9:14).** Thus, Abraham, because of His faith in the living God, also **spiritually** partook of the New Covenant "better blood" of the Lord Jesus through the "wine" Melchizedek ministered to Abraham; and all of its benefits related to purification of conscience and forgiveness of sins.

Hebrews 10:14-18: [14]For by **'first'** offering he hath **'matured' 'into the carried-through,'** them that are sanctified. [15]Whereof **the Holy 'Spirit'** also **is a witness to us:** for after that he had said before, [16]This is the covenant that I will make with them after those days, says the Lord, **I will put my laws into their hearts, and in their minds will I write them;** [17]And their sins and iniquities will I remember **no more.** [18]Now where **'forgiveness'** of these is, there is no more offering for sin.

Hebrews 9:14: How much more shall the **blood of Christ,** who **through the eternal Spirit** offered himself without spot to God, **purge your conscience from dead works to serve the living God?**

Jesus' Blood, Faith, and the Eternal Spirit
With that said, both the bodily sacrifice (the bread) of Jesus and the shedding of His blood (the wine) "matures" the "conscience" of believers in the New Covenant, when these benefits are received by faith **(Heb 10:14-18, Heb 10:1-4, Rom 3:25).** In addition, this maturity of the believers' conscience through the body and blood of our Lord Jesus is witnessed by the **Eternal Holy Spirit.** That is, both the Lord Jesus and the Holy Spirit applies the benefits of the broken body of Jesus and His shed blood in the New Covenant of the Melchizedek's order.

In **Hebrew 10:1-4,** we learn that no animal sacrifice could make those who gave their offerings "mature." The writer also said that if the sacrifices of animals did make them "mature," then they would have "ceased to be offered, because that the worshippers once purged should have not more **conscience** of sins." In other words, the sacrifices of animals and their related shed blood could not reach the conscience of mankind to remove the consciousness of sins!

However, the Lord Jesus' offering of His body and His blood "without spot through the Eternal Spirit," and sprinkling of

His blood, He "matures" our "consciences" purging us from the "consciousness of evil." Thus, we can enter the Holy Places by the blood of Jesus "purging our consciences from dead works to serve the living God." In other words, **if we are not** able to enter into the Holy Places, it is because our consciences are defiled and not purged by the blood of Jesus.

Or, if a believer is not serving God consistently, it may be caused by the lack of proper participation in the communion bread and wine. Through a lack of proper participation in the Lord Supper (taking communion unworthily[13]), some may not be remembering the benefits of the broken body and the blood of Jesus in the New Covenant **(1 Cor 11:27).** Instead, guilt, weakness, death, sickness, condemnation prevails rather than life, health, strength, freedom from guilt, and so on **(1 Cor 11:27-32).**

Hebrews 10:19-22: [19]Having therefore, **brothers,** boldness to enter into the **holy-places by the blood of Jesus,** [20]By a **freshly-slain-sacrifice** and living way, which he has **initiated** for us, through the veil, that is to say, his flesh; [21]And having an high priest over the house of God; [22]Let us draw near with a true heart in full assurance of faith, having our hearts

---

[13] Per **1 Corinthians 11:17-34,** becoming "guilty" of "unworthily" taking the Lord Jesus' Communion is due to some believers getting drunk from the communion wine (they drank real wine and we should also), the richer saints shaming the poorer saints during communion, the richer saints over eating the communion meal (an "expensive" meal by the way), and the richer saints not leaving enough of the meal for the poorer saints, the saints who are more well off than others causing status based division, and so on **(see 1 Cor 12:20-26).**

sprinkled from a '**consciousness of evil,**' and our bodies washed with pure water.

Hebrews 9:12-14: [12]Neither by the blood of goats and calves, but by his own blood he entered in once into the **holy-places,** having obtained eternal redemption for us. [13]For if the blood of bulls and of goats, and the ashes of a heifer sprinkling the unclean, sanctifies to the purifying of the flesh: [14]How much more shall the **blood of Christ**, who **through the eternal Spirit** offered himself without spot to God, **purge your conscience from dead works to serve the living God?**

No Remembrance of Sins

If we cannot serve God properly, it is because our consciences are not purged from dead work (dead works of "sin" and the remembrance of "transgressions"[14] are preventing us from working for and serving the living God). If we keep remembering our sins in our conscience, it is because we have not appropriated the broken body of Jesus, the "first" and "only" needed sacrifice that rids us of the remembrance of sins. This appropriation of Jesus body that was broken for us and His blood that was shed for us is through faith in Him and partaking of bread and wine of communion. That is, God does not remember our sins when we accept the sacrifice of the body of Jesus **(Heb 10:15-18);** and also, because Jesus' sacrifice is "once and for all" time there is no hourly, daily, weekly, monthly, yearly reminder of sins in our lives. In addition, when we partake of the

---

[14] Please refer to my book titled *Her Seed vs his Seed* for further understanding of the difference between "sin," "transgression," and "trespasses"

communion bread and wine, we remember the atonement of Lord Jesus, not our sins.

1 Corinthians 11: 23-25: [23]For I have received of the Lord that which also I delivered unto you, that the Lord Jesus the same night in which he was betrayed took **bread:** [24]And when he had given thanks, he broke it, and said, take, eat: **this is my body, which is broken** for you: this **do in remembrance of me.** [25]After the same manner also he took the cup, when he had supped, saying, this cup is the **New Covenant in my blood:** this do you, as often as you drink it, **in remembrance of me.**

Hebrews 10:1-3: [1]For the law having a shadow of good things to come, and not the very image of the things, can never with those sacrifices which they offered year by year continually make the comers thereunto **'mature.'** [2]For then would they not have ceased to be offered? Because that the worshippers once purged should have had **no more conscience of sins.** [3]But in those sacrifices there is a **remembrance again made of sins every year.** [4]For it is **not possible** that the blood of bulls and of goats should take away sins.

Hebrews 10:8-10: [8]Above when he said, Sacrifice and offering and burnt offerings and offering for sin you willed not, **neither had pleasure therein; which are offered by the law;** [9]Then said he, lo, I come to do your will, O God. He takes away the first, that he may establish the second. [10]By the which will we are **sanctified through the offering of the body of Jesus Christ once for all.**

Hebrews 10:12-18: [12]But this man, after he had offered **'first'** sacrifice for sins **'into the carried-through,'** sat down on the right hand of God; [13]From henceforth expecting **until** his enemies be made his footstool. [14]For by **'first'** offering he hath **'matured' 'into the carried-through,'** them that are sanctified. [15]Whereof the Holy **'Spirit'** also is a witness to us: for after that he had said before, [16]This is the covenant that I will make with them after those days, says the Lord, **I will put my laws into their hearts, and in their minds will I write them;** [17]And their sins and iniquities will I remember **no more.** [18]Now where **'forgiveness'** of these is, there is no more offering for sin.

Communion and Uncircumcised Abram

Thus, when Melchizedek met "Abram" (while "Abram" was still uncircumcised and God had not changed his name yet to "Abraham"), Melchizedek administer the body and the blood (bread and wine) of the Lord Jesus to the conscience of Abram purging dead works and the consciousness of evil that hurt others (i.e., the war[15] he and his men was just engaged in). Abram, while in uncircumcision (a symbol representing being unsaved and a heathen) partook of the New Covenant in the blood of Jesus.

Abram, while in uncircumcision (a symbol of considered being unsaved and a heathen), partook of the broken body of Jesus in which God purged any consciousness his sins! All these principles are true and apply to the Jesus' order of Melchizedek, both now and eternally. Every uncircumcised person, (non-Jews according to the flesh) and every

---

[15] The "better blood" of the Lord Jesus can help to heal the consciences of veterans of war who have shed blood in the heat of war. You may refer to my first book, *Melchizedek,* under the chapter titled "Melchizedek and War" for further reading.

circumcised person (Jews according to the flesh), can partake of the New Covenant body and blood of Jesus Christ

Ephesians 2:11-21: [11]Therefore, remember that you being in time past **Gentiles** in the flesh, who are called **Uncircumcision** by that which is called the **Circumcision in the flesh made by hands;** [12]That at that time you were without Christ, being aliens from the commonwealth of Israel, and strangers from the covenants of promise, having no hope, and without God in the world: [13]But now in Christ Jesus you who sometimes were far off are made **near** by the **blood of Christ**. [14]For he is our peace, who has **made both one**, and has broken down the middle wall of partition between us; [15]Having abolished in his flesh the enmity, even the law of commandments contained in ordinances; for to make in himself of **two, one new man,** so making peace; [16]And that he might reconcile both unto God in one body by the cross, having slain the enmity thereby: [17]And came and preached peace to you which were afar off, and to them that were **near.** [18]For through him we both have **access by one Spirit** unto the Father. [19]Now therefore you are no more strangers and foreigners, but fellow-citizens with the saints, and of the household of God; [20]And are built upon the foundation of the apostles and prophets, Jesus Christ himself being the chief corner stone; [21]In whom all the building fitly framed together grows unto a holy temple in the Lord: [22]In whom you also are **built** together for a habitation of God through the Spirit.

Our conscience is purged by the blood of Jesus; and it is reinforced by our continual partaking of the Lord's communion. In the taking of the New Covenant communion "we remember" the Lord's "body which was broken for us," reminding us that through the Jesus sacrifice of His body, God does not remember our sins. We **"remember"** the Lord's **"New 'Covenant' in His blood,"** reminding us that our consciences are purged from the dead works of sins and transgressions.

1 Corinthians 11:25: After the same manner also he took the cup, when he had supped, saying, this cup is the **New Covenant in my blood: this** do you, as often as you drink it, in remembrance of me.

Hebrews 10:15-17: [15]Whereof the Holy **'Spirit'** also is a witness to us: for after that he had said before, [16]This is **the covenant** that I will make with them after those days .... [17]And their sins and iniquities will I remember **no more.** [18]Now where **'forgiveness'** of these is, there is no more offering for sin.

Hebrews 9:14: How much more shall the **blood of Christ,** who **through the eternal Spirit** offered himself without spot to God, **purge your conscience from dead works** to serve the living God?

MELCHIZEDEK AND OUR CONSCIENCES

Interpretation-Jesus' Blood is Better

Hebrews 9:12-14: [12]Neither by the blood of goats and calves, but **by his own blood he entered in once into the holy-places,** having obtained eternal redemption for us. [13]For if the blood of bulls and of goats, and the ashes of a heifer sprinkling the unclean, sanctifies to the purifying of the flesh: [14]How much more shall the blood of Christ, who through the eternal Spirit offered himself without spot to God, **purge your conscience** from dead works to serve the living God?

Hebrews 10:19-22: [19]Having therefore, brothers, boldness to **enter into the holy-places by the blood of Jesus,** [20]By a freshly-slain-sacrifice and living way, which he has initiated for us, through the veil, that is to say, his flesh; [21]And having an high priest over the house of God; [22]Let us draw near with a true heart in full assurance of faith, **having our hearts sprinkled from a 'consciousness of evil,'** and our bodies washed with pure water.

It seemed good to the Holy Spirit and me to utilize additional writing to also briefly bring out benefits that relate to the conscience of all believers that were gifted to us through Jesus' Melchizedek's more excellent ministry **(Heb 8:6).** That is, the more excellent ministry of Jesus' Melchizedek order is within the New Covenant that was established upon "better promises." One of the better promises is that upon accepting the offering of the sacrifice and blood of the Lord Jesus and receiving the heavenly Father's forgiveness through the same, the Heavenly Father does **not remember** our "sins" and "lawlessness" **(Heb 8:12).**

Another of the better promises of the New Covenant is that the blood of Jesus, that was shed "once" and applied to our conscience, through faith in Jesus' blood, also causes us not to remember our sins or be conscious of sins, because Jesus' sacrifice and blood removes sin form our consciences **(Heb 10:3-4 w/Heb 10:10-18, Heb 9:12-14, Heb 10:19-22)**. This, then brings me to highlight one of the better benefits of Jesus' Melchizedek order. Jesus' blood was/is applied simultaneously to our consciences when He sprinkled the Tabernacle in heaven some two thousand years ago and His sacrifice and blood is as fresh today as it was then when applied to our conscience!

The Holy Places and Our Consciences
In **Hebrew 9:12-14** we read that the Lord Jesus Christ "by his **own blood** he entered in once into the **holy-places,** having obtained eternal redemption for us." In the same "God-breathed" writing we see that our "consciences" are simultaneous "purged" with the same blood. "How much more shall the **blood of Christ,** who through the eternal Spirit offered himself without spot to God, **purge your conscience.**" In other words, the Holy Places in heaven have a spiritual symmetric equal in believing humans, the consciences of the saints (God's corporate human tabernacles on earth and in heaven). That is, your consciences are also considered God's Holy Places that Jesus Himself entered and sprinkled with His blood to purge it so you can serve the living God! Because, Jesus' believers are "the Temple of God," bodily (He dwells in us individually by His Spirit); and we are "the Temple of God" corporately; as Jesus' blood was sprinkled in the Temple of the Tabernacle in heaven, so His blood is sprinkled in the Temple of our

bodies (our hearts or consciences)-**1 Cor 3:16, 1 Cor 6:19, 2 Cor 6:16-18, Heb 9:21-23, Heb 10:21-22**

This truth is again reinforced in **Hebrews 10:19-22,** where it is said, "Having therefore, brothers, boldness to enter into the **holy-places** by the **blood of Jesu**s ... having our **hearts** sprinkled from a **'consciousness'** of evil' ...." These words are similar to **Hebrews 9:12-14,** upon the mentioning of Jesus' blood and the Holy Places, the conscience is simultaneously referenced. In other words, the consciences of believers can be synonymous with the Holy Places in heaven. This is one of the principles of the Melchizedek order that is difficult to interpret, and in order to receive this, a believer must not be "sluggish to hear," and also have their senses trained to discern between good and evil **(Heb 5:10-14).** One of the purposes of our consciences being purged by the blood of the Lord Jesus Christ is to "serve the living Gd" after the powerful blood of Jesus "purified our consciences from dead works."

In case you did not know, the great Apostle Paul had to have his conscience purged by the blood of Jesus, just as us **(1 Tim 3:9).** And his conscience was so "matured" through the blood of Jesus, according to the Melchizedek order, that Paul boldly declared himself to walk "maturely" in one of the benefits of the New Covenant. Paul **"was not 'conscious' of anything against himself"**[16] **(1 Cor 4:4).** In other words, Paul was fully wearing in faith the benefit of the sacrifice and the blood of Jesus. This benefit is the heavenly Father does not

---

[16] Paul not being conscious of anything against himself does not mean a believer does not acknowledge reality of his/her past of ignorant actions, which helps to keep us humble (1 Tim 1:13, 1 Tim 1:15, 1 Cor 15:9).

remember our sins and lawlessness once He forgives us through the blood of Jesus; and we also are **no more conscious** of evil or conscious of sins **(1 Cor 4:4 w/Heb 8:12 w/Heb 10:17-18).**

Hebrews 9:12-15: [12]Neither by the blood of goats and calves, but **by his own blood he entered in once into the holyplaces,** having obtained **eternal redemption** for us. [13]For if the blood of bulls and of goats, and the ashes of a heifer sprinkling the unclean, sanctifies to the purifying of the flesh: [14]How much more shall the blood of Christ, who through the eternal Spirit offered himself without spot to God, **purge your conscience** from dead works to serve the living God? [15]**And for this reason** He is the Mediator of the New Covenant, by means of death, for **the redemption of the transgressions** under the **first covenant**, that those who are called may receive the **promise of the eternal inheritance.**

Eternal Inheritance

In addition to what was just discussed above, it is important to note that a person with a conscience that is not purged or purified by the blood of Jesus Christ cannot partake of Jesus eternal inheritance, the eternal redemption **(Heb 9:12, 15).** The transgression of the people who were under the previous covenant prevented them from having "eternal inheritance" of "eternal redemption," because the blood of bulls, goats, sheep cannot purge sin in the conscience **(see also Heb 10).** Therefore, all who transgressed under the previous covenant could not inherit. They had to wait until Jesus came and offered the better sacrifice of Himself. Jesus' blood purified both sins of the past, present sins, and all future sins. Therefore, no more sacrifice for sins is needed forever **(Heb 10:10 w/Heb 10:17).**

As a result of Jesus sacrifices, those who were held in Abraham's Bosom were able to join the Lord Jesus Christ in the heavens, because their conscience was purified through the **"blood of the 'eternal' Covenant,"** the blood of the Lord Jesus and His eternal Spirit **(Heb 13:18-20)**. Because **"the blood of Christ,** who through the **eternal Spirit** offered himself without spot to God, purged [our] conscience ... **for this reason** He is the Mediator of the New Covenant, by means of death, for the **redemption of the transgressions under the first covenant**, that **those who are called** may **receive the promise of the eternal inheritance."**

With respect to this truth outlined above, **Hebrews 11:40** also said that those in the Old Covenant, who did walk by faith with the living God, could not be matured without us, **"God having provided some better thing for us, that they without us should not be made 'matured' (Heb 11:40).** This "maturity" can be applied to what the book of Hebrews defines as a "mature conscience," through the applied blood of Jesus that atoned for sins. That is, Jesus' Melchizedek order, which is an eternal priesthood, who is "carried-through" into heaven, 'into the age" also purged the conscience of the Old Testament saints of all sin consciousness (called a "matured conscience") to now be allowed with Him in the heavens, as well as the New Covenant saints (those alive in Christ and those who sleep in Christ) who also now have a "matured conscience" through the blood of Jesus **(contracts Heb 10:2 w/Heb 9:14 w/Heb 10:20-22).**

Jesus' blood is that powerful to also apply to the Old Covenant saints and also continues to apply **now** to the New Covenant saints, some two thousand years from when He walked the earth in flesh and blood. The purging of the conscience is that important that without Jesus' blood we could not receive the eternal inheritance of eternal redemption through the eternal Covenant! Thus, Jesus paid the price to free our consciences to inherit life with Christ eternally with our spirit and soul until the full redemption of our bodies, us being "placed" as "sons" in resurrected bodies **(Rom 8:23 w/Eph 1:14 w/Heb 9:12-15).**

Please be reminded that all the application of the blood of the Lord Jesus is still being administered by the eternal Holy Spirit. The **blood of Jesus** and **the eternal Spirit** are inseparable. **"The Spirit bears witness to the Truth;"** and **"the Spirit, the water and the blood, these three are into the one"** **(1 John 5:6; 5:8).** With all that was said, in this section, let us now review scriptures related to the conscience.

Good Conscience

Acts 23:1 And Paul, earnestly beholding the council, said, men and brethren, I have **lived** in all **good conscience** before God until this day.

1. "Lived" is the Greek word politeoumai; and it is defined as citizen, policy, polite.
    a. For example, the apostle Paul lived as a polite citizen of God's kingdom.
2. Conscience means "joint-knowing," co-perception, co-seeing, co-knowing, a knowing-together, self-judging consciousness.
3. "Good" is translated from the Greek word "agathos;" and it means inherent (intrinsic) good.
    a. The Lord Jesus said, there is none good except God **(Luke 18:19)**. Thus, a good nature is God's nature. We demonstrate this good nature of God by doing God's

commandments of loving God and loving your neighbors-**Matt 19:16-26**

4. The apostle Paul made it clear to the council who is about to judge him unjustly that he "lived in all **'intrinsic good'** conscience before God until that day."

   a. Once our consciences are purged by the better blood of our Lord Jesus, we should maintain a beautiful or attractive intrinsically good conscience before the living God as we serve Him!

Conscience Void of Offences

Acts 24:15-16: [15]And have hope toward God, which they themselves also allow, that **there shall be a resurrection of the dead, both of the just and unjust.** [16]**And herein** do I **exercise** myself, to have always a **conscience void of offence** toward God, and toward men.

1. Due to the **surety** of resurrection of the dead, both of the just and the unjust, Paul practiced **adorning** his conscience to be void of offence.

2. The word exercise, cited above, means to form by art, to adorn, to take pains, to labor, to strive, to elaborate, to train.

   a. The conscience can be **trained** or **adorned** not to offend (strike) God and men.

5. Conscience means "joint-knowing," co-perception, co-seeing, co-knowing, a knowing-together, self-judging consciousness.

6. The phrase "void of offence" is a compound word in the Greek made up of alpha (as a negative prefix) and pro (towards) and skopto (cut, incised resulting in severance, being cut off, mourn)

a. Like the apostle Paul, due to the surety of the resurrection of the dead, wherein all will also be judged according to their conscience, we are to adorn ourselves with a conscience that does not "strike-towards" God or man.

b. We are not to "cut off" God or man in our consciences due to offences.

c. Conscience void of **offence** is realized by "abounding (in) love" as we increase **"in knowledge"** and increase **"in all 'sensing'"**-Phil 1:9-10

   i. As we increase "in knowledge," of God and His Melchizedek order, we are to abound in love, because "knowledge puff up, but love edifies"-**Phil 1:9-10 w/1 Cor 8:1 w/1 Cor 13:4**

      1. God's love in us will cause us not to strike at God or man when we increase in knowledge. "Love is kind"-**1 Cor 13:4**

   ii. As we increase in "all sensing," able to understand the mature teaching concerning Jesus' Melchizedek order, we are to abound in love, because developed senses that discerns and judges all things must be tempered with love, least we disapprove God's "excellent" things that looks "different" from what we are acquainted with-**Phil 1:9-10 w/Heb 5:14 w/Heb 8:6**

      1. God's love in us will cause us not to strike at God or strike at each other when we walk in "all sensing" (knowing the intent of a person (good or evil)-**1 Cor 13:5-7, w/Heb 4:12-1, 1 John 2:20, 1 Cor 2:15**

         a. **Note**: Developed senses attained through the living God that enable discernment in us is to be used for maturing us in the things of God; it is to be used to protect us from Antichrist and antichrists spirits; it is to be used to teach us to be prudent, etc.-**John 2:23-25, I John 2:20, Heb 5:14**

Conscience Bearing Witnesses

Romans 2:15: Which show the work of the **law written in their hearts,** their **conscience** also **bearing witness,** and their **thoughts** the mean while **accusing or else excusing** one another).

1. In the New Covenant of the Lord Jesus' Melchizedek order the law is now written in our hearts and deep thoughts of both Jews and Gentiles believers-**Rom 2:14, Heb 8:10-13, Heb 10:15-18**
2. Conscience means "joint-knowing," co-perception, co-seeing, co-knowing, a knowing-together, self-judging consciousness.
3. The conscience also bears witness **in us** to what is true-**Rom 9:1, 2 Cor 1:12**
4. Accuse is the Greek compound "kata" and "agoreuo" which means to speak in an assembly, accuse in an assembly, transliterated "categorize" (place in a group by accusations)-**Rev 12:10**
5. Excusing is the Greek compound "apo" and "logo;" and excusing means to give account of oneself, legal plea, defending oneself (through the Word (logo)
6. The conscience bears witness to the truth by our thoughts (internal reasoning) either **"accusing"** or **"defending"** one another.

Giving and the Conscience

Romans 13:5-7 [5]Therefore you must needs be **subject,** not only for **wrath,** but also for **conscience's sake.** [6]'**Because,**'

through this, **pay** you **tribute** also: **for they are God's ministers, attending continually** upon this very thing. [7]**'Give-from'** therefore to all their **dues: tribute** to whom tribute is due; **custom** to whom custom; **fear** to whom fear; **honor** to whom honor.

1. Subject is defined as submitting to God's ministers of Jesus' Melchizedek's order.
2. Wrath is understood to mean that God's minister may exercise wrath against those who "practice" evil-**Rom 13:4, Rev 15**
   a. God's ministers can exercise wrath through using the sword of the Word of God-**Rom 13:4, Eph 6:17, Acts 13:6-12**
   b. We are to be subjected to God's ministers for wrath's sake because they bear not the sword of the Word of God in vain.
3. Conscience means "joint-knowing," co-perception, co-seeing, co-knowing, a knowing-together, self-judging consciousness.
4. The phrase "for conscience's sake" means that in Jesus' Melchizedek order, we are to submit to God's ministers, not only because of potential wrath, but for conscience's sake.
   a. Our consciences either accuses or defends us.
5. The phrase, "because, through this pay you tribute" means that saints should "pay yearly tribute completion" to the ministers of God in the Melchizedek order.
6. Attending continually speak to God's ministers who "towards-govern" themselves to God's word consistently.
   a. God ministers (I emphasize, God's genuine birthed minister) are **"governed-towards"** the ministry of God

according to the order of Melchizedek-**see Greek words and definitions of Acts 6:4**

7. The phrase "their dues" means "they owed;" thus, ministers of God are owed their dues for the work of the ministry-**1 Tim 5:17-18**

8. Tribute, custom, fear honor are four (4) of the things that are due to God's ministers.

    a. Tribute of their yearly pay for God's ministers

    b. Custom means completion of tolls

    c. Fear speaks of a healthy fear (respect) of God's ministers.

    d. Honor according to the Greek definition speaks of valuing God's ministers with honor, as we value money.

Idols and Consciences

1 Corinthian 8:7: However, there is **not in every man that knowledge:** for some with **'habit'** of the idol unto this hour eat it as a thing offered unto an idol; and their **conscience being weak is defiled.**

1. Not every man has the knowledge to know that even though there are many idols, to believer with the knowledge of God, there is only one God and one Lord, the God and Father of our Lord Jesus Christ

2. Conscience means "joint-knowing," co-perception, co-seeing, co-knowing, a knowing-together, self-judging consciousness.

3. The conscience being weak speaks of idol worship that reduces the effectiveness of the conscience's ability to guide a person relative to the truth of the living God.

    a. Any form of idol worship (covetousness, worship of phantoms, worship of demons, silver, gold, brass) weaken the conscience to be subject to the **demons** behind the idols, through their habitual practices **(1 Cor 10:20).**

4. Defile means to stain; and therefore, in addition to being weaken by idol worship the conscience can also be stained-**Titus 1:15**

    i. Consciences being defiled can happen through:

        1. Idols-**1 Cor 8:7**

        2. Bitterness-**Heb 12:15 w/Titus 1:15**

        3. Dreams (i.e., impure dreams through improper sexuality)-**Jude 1:7-8 w/Titus 1:15**

            a. Dreams through Baal (Satan)-**Jer 23:13 w/Jer 23:27 w/Matt 12:24-26** (where Jesus equates Baal with Satan)

      b. Only the "sprinkling" of better blood of Jesus in our consciences can purify the conscience from weakness, stains, low self-esteem, etc.-**Heb 9:14, Heb 12:24, 1 Pet 1:2, Isaiah 52:14-53:2.**

Wounded and Weak Consciences

1 Corinthians 8:10-12: [10]For if any man sees you which has knowledge sit at meat in the idol's temple, shall not the **conscience** of him which is weak be **emboldened** to eat those things which are offered to idols; [11]And through your knowledge shall the **weak** brother perish, for whom Christ died? [12]But when you sin so against the brethren, and **wound** their **weak conscience**, you sin against Christ.

1. Conscience means "joint-knowing," co-perception, co-seeing, co-knowing, a knowing-together, self-judging consciousness.

2. The phrase, the **"conscience** of him which is **weak can** be **emboldened** means the following:

a. Habitual idol worship weakens the conscience to continue in its sin-**1 Cor 8:7**

b. Embolden means "house-building," to build up someone.

   i. Thus, if a person who has knowledge that idols are in reality nothing eats meat sacrifice to idols in the idols' temple, and the person with the "weak conscience" sees it, the weak conscience will be embolden again to eat things sacrificed to idols which in turn defiles the weak conscience again and it is considered "sin against the [weak] brother" and "sin against Christ."

   ii. The remedy on behalf of the brothers or sisters with the weak conscience is to refrain from eating such in the presence of them-**please read 1 Cor 10:23-33**

3. **Wound** their weak **conscience.**

a. Wound means to "thump" repeatedly, to strike repeatedly, to beat repeatedly.

b. If another brother or sister who has knowledge eat things sacrificed to idols, a person with a "weak conscience" can be "wounded" by being "thumped repeatedly" to be "embolden" (lit., home-building) worship to idols and worship of the spirits behind the idols -**1 Cor 10:25-33 w/1 Cor 8:10**

   i. Remember, because idols and the eating related to idols are considered as "nothing" to the believer who knows that the living Father of the Lord Jesus is the "only" God, it is not sin to this knowledgeable person to eat-**1 Cor 8:4-8**

   ii. However, a believer who is weak to idols, whose conscience is defiled, can be thumped back into idol worship through misunderstanding the stronger brother's action.

  iii. This then results in the stronger brother or sister sinning against and thumping the weaker conscience of his brother or sister.

  iv. Therefore, the stronger should abstain for conscience's sake, the conscience of the weaker brother or sister-**1 Cor 10:27-33, 1 Cor 8:13, 1 Cor 10**

Cauterized Conscience

1 Timothy 4:1-2: [1]Now the **Spirit speaks expressly,** that in the **latter times** some shall **depart from the faith, giving heed** to seducing spirits, and doctrines of devils; [2]**Speaking lies in hypocrisy;** having their **conscience seared with a hot iron.**

1. The expression, "the Spirit speaks expressly" is better translated as "the Spirit speaks 'explicitly.'

2. The phrase "latter times" means "under-seasons."

  a. The world is currently "under" a "season" of intense lies being propagated by seducing spirit and demonic teachings, just as the Holy Spirit explicitly said it would happen.

3. The expression "depart from the faith" prophetically speaks of the "apostacy" or "divorce" from the faith.

  a. Depart mean to "from-stand," it is associated with falling away ("apostacy") before the man of lawlessness is revealed-**2 Thes 2:3**; and it is associated with the Greek word for "divorce" due to hardness of heart-**Mat 19:7**; and is also associated with "departing" from the living God through bitterness and being unpersuadable of God-**Heb 3:12**

    i. Some shall fall away, divorce, depart from "the Faith" (the way and faith of our Lord Jesus Christ) to become "holding-ones" of teachings of demons and seducing spirits.

4. The words "giving heed" means "holding ones" according to the Greek definition.

    a. "Giving heed" is more serious than written by the King James Version

    b. "Giving heed" means to become "towards-holders" of teaching of demons and wandering spirits.

        i. We are to be "holders" of the Holy Spirit of Christ-**Rom 8:9**

        ii. We are **not** to become holding ones of the teaching of demons and seducing spirits.

5. Seducing spirits and doctrines of demons

    a. Seducing spirits are the antichrist spirits who are against the Spirit of Truth-**1 John 4:6**

    b. Doctrines of demons

        i. People are used to hearing of spirits seducing humanity-**2 John 1:7;** however, they are not acute to the fact that demons also teach through those who "holds" demons and those who have their conscience cauterized. Yes, demons from the Devil teach lies through people-**John 8:44, Rev 16:13-14, etc.**

6. Speaking lies in hypocrisy.

    a. Per the Greek reading of **1 Timothy 4:1-2,** those who depart from the faith and become holding-ones of seducing spirits and holders of demonic teaching through hearing lies spoken in hypocrisy, occurs after their "conscience" have been "cauterized" "set on fire" or "branded" by these spirits and demons!

7. Conscience means "joint-knowing," co-perception, co-seeing, co-knowing, a knowing-together, self-judging consciousness.

8. A "conscience seared with a hot iron" means people will be "'cauterized' in their own conscience."

    a. The words "seared with a hot iron" are translated from the Greek word "kauteriazo," transliterated as "cauterized." Cauterized is from a root word meaning to burn or set on fire.

    b. Through the fire produced by seducing spirits and the fire produced by demons in their teachings, these fires can "sear" the conscience to be become insensitive to what is true.

        i. Remember the conscience bears witness (give evidence and testifies of what it has seen is true)

        ii. Thus, a seared or branded conscience cannot discern truth; and thus, believes the seducing spirits and teaching of demons instead of God's truth; and the person with the seared conscience also become "holding ones" of these same seducing spirits and demons.

Answer of a Good Conscience

1 Peter 3:19-21: [19]By which also **he went and preached unto the spirits in prison;** [20]Which sometime were **disobedient,** when once the longsuffering of God waited in the days of Noah, while the ark was a preparing, wherein few, that is, **eight souls were saved by water.** [21]The like figure whereunto even **baptism** does also now **save us** (not the putting away of the filth of the flesh, but the **answer of a good conscience toward God,) by the resurrection of Jesus Christ.**

1. Jesus Christ "went and preached[17] to the spirits in prison." That is, the Lord Jesus in His death, before His resurrection, preached to the imprisoned spirits which were **"unpersuaded"** in the days of Noah before the flood.
2. Eight souls were saved by water in the days of Noah. Noah, his wife, his three sons and their wives were saved by the same water that destroyed those who were unpersuaded of the cataclysm by water that was about to happen in their day.
3. Apostle Peter revealed that the phrase "saved by water" represents water baptism that also saves those who believe in Jesus.
4. Per apostle Peter, Baptism in Christ is **not only** for removing dirt from our flesh-**Heb 10:22 w/1 Peter 3:19-21.** Baptism is God's response to the demand and inquiry related to having a good conscience "into God."
5. Peter's statement of "good conscience by the resurrection of Jesus" represents Jesus' resurrection that causes water baptism to have an effect on our consciences (washing our consciences from accusations, defilements, weaknesses, and wounds we briefly discussed in this section)
   a. In other words, water baptism washed our bodies **(Heb 10:22); and** water baptism washes our consciences **(1 Pet 3:21)**

Conscience and the Blood of Christ
Hebrews 9:11-14: [11]But **Christ** being come a **High Priest** of **good things to come,** by a **greater and more perfect**

---

[17] You may refer to my book *The Prophetic Patterns of the Two Witnesses* for further development of this truth

tabernacle, not made with hands, that is to say, not of this '**creation;'** [12]Neither by the blood of goats and calves, but by **his own blood** he entered in once into the '**holy places,'** having obtained **eternal redemption** for us. [13]For if the blood of bulls and of goats, and the ashes of a heifer sprinkling the unclean, sanctifies to the purifying of the flesh: [14]How much more shall the **blood of Christ,** who **through the eternal Spirit offered himself without spot to God, purge** your **conscience** from **dead works** to **serve the living God**?

1. The principle of "Christ being come a High Priest" speaks of the Lord Jesus who is High Priest according to the order of Melchizedek-**Heb 7 w/Heb 8:1**
2. The "good things to come" are all of the better benefits of the New Covenant. For example, the good thing of Jesus' better blood that matures the conscience from remembering sins God have forgiven-**Heb 10**
3. Greater and more 'mature' tabernacle is the heavenly tabernacle and the tabernacle of Jesus' fleshly body.
   a. The literal "true" heavenly "Tabernacle"-**Heb 8:1-6, Heb 9:23-24, Rev 15:5-18, Rev 11:19**
   b. Jesus, "the Word became flesh and '**Tabernacled'** among us" - **John 1:14**
   c. God's tabernacle is also the "City," New Jerusalem-**Rev 21:3**
      i. Believers are also a "city laid on a 'mountain'"-**Mat 5:14**
   d. God's tabernacle is "those in heaven tabernacling"-**Rev 13:6**
      i. **Rev 13:6**, in the oldest Greek text read: "And he opened his mouth in blasphemy against God, to blaspheme his name, and **his tabernacle, 'those who tabernacled' in heaven."**

1. **Yes, God's "tabernacle" is "those who tabernacled in heaven," and thus His "Tabernacle" has manifold manifestations-see also Rev 12:12**

4. Christ's ... own blood is applied to our conscience.
   a. The blood of animals could **not** remove sins permanently and thus **not** able to make the conscience matured; the blood of animals could only purify the flesh temporarily -**Heb 10, Heb 9:13**
   b. Only the blood of Jesus, who offered Himself to God without spot, can purge sins permanently-**Heb 9:14, Heb 10:19-22, Heb 12:24, Heb 10:16-18, etc.**

5. The holy places are the holy places of the tabernacle in heaven and the holy places of our consciences simultaneously-**Heb 9:11 w/Heb 9:14 w/Heb 10:19-22**
   a. This simultaneous purifying of the holy places in the heavens and the holy places in our consciences was accomplished through Jesus and the Eternal Pure Spirit-**Heb 9:14 w/1 John 5:6**
   b. Because we are "the Temple of God," bodily (He dwells in us individually by His Spirit); and we are "the Temple of God" corporately; as Jesus' blood was sprinkled in the Temple of the Tabernacle in heaven, so His blood is sprinkled in the Temple of our bodies (our hearts or consciences)-**1 Cor 3:16, 1 Cor 6:19, 2 Cor 6:16-18, Heb 9:21-23, Heb 10:21-22**

6. Eternal Redemption is through Jesus' Blood
   a. The Lord Jesus' sacrifice and offering of His blood to God are the only things that can "covenant" eternal redemption into eternal inheritance.
   b. Through the "price" of blood of the Lord Jesus all believers who were under the Old Covenant and the New Covenant are **eternally** "loosed" from the hold of

the Devil, Sin, Death, and Hell- **Acts 2:24, Rev 1:18, Heb 2:14-15, Rom 6:9, etc.**

    i. The Lord Jesus captured captivity (death and hell) and freed the saints who were in Abraham's Bosom to now be with Him **(Eph 4:8, Col 2:15, Luke 16:19-31, Matt 27:50-53, 2 Cor 5:6-8)**

c. Through the shed blood of our Lord Jesus Christ all the saints from the Old Covenant, who were being held in Abraham's Bosom, were allowed to inherit eternally being transported with the Lord Jesus to be with Him in the heavens in Christ-**Luke 16:22 w/Heb 9:15, Matt 27:50-53, etc.**

d. Through the shed blood of our Lord Jesus Christ, all the saints of the New Covenant eternally inherit to include but not limited to always be with Christ whether we are here on earth or we fall asleep (die)-**Phil 1:21-25, 2 Cor 5:6-9, Rom 14:8, 1 Thes 4:14, etc.**

7. The Eternal Spirit and the Blood of Jesus

a. Our Lord Jesus Christ is one with the Eternal Spirit of the heavenly Father (God is Spirit!)-**John 4:24, Mat 10:29, 1 John 5:8**

b. The Spirit of the heavenly Father was "into" Jesus; the Lord Jesus was "into" the heavenly Father, as the Son-**Heb 1:4, Mat 10:20**

8. Who through the Eternal Spirit offered Himself without spot to God.

a. The Eternal Spirit led the Lord Jesus in "holy-togetherness;" therefore, there was **no** blemish of sin in the Lord Jesus-**Rom 1:4, Heb 9:14, Heb 7:26**

b. All believers must also be sanctified by the Holy Spirit-**1 Pet 1:2, Rom 15:16, 1 Cor 6:11**

9. Conscience means "joint-knowing," co-perception, co-seeing, co-knowing, knowing-together, self-judging consciousness.
10. Our conscience is purged through Jesus' better blood.
    a. Our conscience (joint-knowing) relative to sins can only be purged and purified through the better blood of the Lord Jesus Christ
        i.   We are admonished to hold the mystery of faith in pure conscience that is only purged through Jesus' blood-**1 Tim 3:9**
        ii. This can mean that if the conscience becomes impure again, by rejecting the Lord Jesus and His better blood, the mystery of the faith may not be "held" in one's heart and thus causing a falling away-**1 Tim 4:1-2, Heb 10:26-26**
        iii. The apostle Paul indicated that serving God with a pure conscience involves prayer-**2 Tim 1:3**
             1. Hence, one of the ways we serve the living God after our consciences are purged is in prayer to God on behalf of others.
11. Dead Works
    a. Dead works can mean works of sins, transgressions, and trespasses-**Eph 2:1, Col 2:13**
    b. Before we received Jesus' blood through His grace by faith "we were dead in **trespasses** and **sin**" -**Eph 2:1**
    c. Trespass is the Greek compound word "para" (besides, near) and "ptoma" (to fall), which means falling from God's love into satanic "fear."
        i.   Adam "besides-fell" from God's love and fell into fear.
        ii. Since "love never falls," and there is not fear in love, and mature love cast out fear, Adam's

"beside-fall" was that he left God's "love" and "fell" into "fear"-**1 Cor 13:8 w/1 John 4:18, w/Gen 3:10**

d. Sins comes from the Greek word "harmatria" and means to miss the mark so as not to share in the prize, the "un-allotted," the un-shared, un-portioned

   i. The tree of the knowledge of good and evil was "not-shared" and "not-allotted" to Adam and Eve.

   ii. Hence, part of their sin was they ate from the tree that was "not-allotted" and "un-shared" to them. Therefore, they did not partake of the prize of eating from the tree of eternal life at that time.

12. Serve the living God.

    a. Serving the living God includes but not limited to praying to God-**Luke 2:37, Rom 1:9**

    b. Serving the living God includes but not limited to serving His Tabernacle-**i.e., Heb 13:10**

    c. This serving is to be done "in the Spirit" of God and with our spirit-**Phil 3:3, Rom 1:9, 1 Cor 14:14, Matt 26:41, John 11:43 w/Rom 8:26, Isaiah 26:9, Rom 8:16, Jude 1:20, etc.**

In conclusion of this section, your consciences are considered Holy Places of the living God. The blood of Jesus is also applied there (to your consciences). Thus, the Apostle Paul have exhorted believers, who now have purified consciences, to endeavor to have a conscience that does not strike at God or man **(Acts 24:16)**. Let us serve the living God with a "pure conscience" "as in heaven so on earth!" Part of our eternal inheritance, the eternal redemption is directly linked to the blood of Jesus sprinkled into our consciences according to the order of Melchizedek!

MELCHIZEDEK ORDER PRIEST-WORKERS

Interpretation-Practices of Melchizedek

This section exegete scriptures that shows some of the practices of the Melchizedek order. As in, preaching the gospel of God is considered as "priest-working" in the order of Melchizedek. Preaching the gospel is equated to working in the "priest-temple;" and preaching the gospel is also equated to those who attend the altar in the "priest-temple;" and thus, "the Lord ordained that they which preach the gospel should live of the gospel."[18] It will also be exegeted to show that "fit" elder women "priests" are to teach the younger wives or women behavior that relates to the orderly conducts of the Melchizedek order in marriage, so that the word of God be not blasphemed. And we will also exegete the Apostle Peter's teaching on the Melchizedek order.

Romans 15:15-16-Priest-Workers

[15]Nevertheless, brethren, I have written the more boldly unto you in some sort, as putting you in mind, because of the grace that is given to me of God, [16]That I should be the **minister** of Jesus Christ to the Gentiles, **ministering the gospel of God,** that the **offering up of the Gentiles** might be acceptable, being **sanctified by the Holy Spirit.**

1. The word "minister" (Greek: "leitourgos") is a Greek compound which means "people-worker," "worker" on behalf of the "people."
2. The other word translated as ministering (hierourgeó) is also a Greek compound which means "priest-worker," a "priest" who "works" on behalf of God for the people.

---

[18] **Note:** as we discussed the importance of conscience in the previous section, giving or a lack thereof, affects the conscience **(Rom 13:5-7).**

a. Paul is an apostle priest-worker.

  i. Apostles, prophets, evangelist, pastors and teachers, spiritual persons are of the high "priesthood" of the Melchizedek order.

b. Hence, all of Jesus' "apostles of the Lamb" and "apostles of Christ" are also Melchizedek order priests of God.

c. All the "royal priesthood" consisting of God's believer are also "priest-workers" in the Melchizedek order-**1 Pet 2:9**

  i. However, in the priesthood, there are different level of ministers and ministries.

  ii. In the Old Covenant Levitical priesthood, through the tribe of Levi, there exist the high priests through Aaron (with their "service" and "warfare"); then the high priests' sons (with their "service" and "warfare"); then the Levites (with their "service" and "warfare"), the kingdom of the priesthood of the people in general-**Ex 19:6**

  iii. In the everlasting New Covenant, through the Tribe of the Lord Jesus, the tribe of Judah, there is the order of Melchizedek High-Priest, the Son, the Lord Jesus; there is Jesus' Melchizedek priesthood of sons (apostolic sons, prophetic sons, teacher sons, evangelist sons, pastoral sons, spiritual sons and spiritual daughters, baby sons and daughters, young adult sons and daughters, and mature sons and daughters, etc.).

3. Ministering the gospel of God means priest-working in the gospel of God according to the order of Melchizedek.

4. The phrase "offering up of the Gentiles" are the people of the nations who are converted by the Melchizedek's priesthood and considered an "offerings to God."

5. Sanctified by the Holy Spirit means it is the Holy Spirit who cleanse all believer to be acceptable to God.
    a. It is through the eternal Spirit Jesus offered Himself to God without spot-**Heb 9:14**
    b. It is through the Holy Spirit it is witnessed that God does not remember our sins through the offering of the sacrifice of Jesus-**Heb 10:14-18**
    c. So likewise, it is the Holy Spirit who internally cleans the Gentiles believer to be offered acceptable to God-**Rom 15:16, Isaiah 66:20-21**

1 Cor 9:13-14-The Altar of Preaching
1 Corinthians 9:13-14: [13]Do you not know that they which **minister** about **holy things** live of the things of the temple? And they which **wait** at the altar are **partakers** with **the altar?** [14]**Even so** has the Lord **ordained** that they which preach the gospel should live of the gospel.

1. The word minister, in the reference above, is the Greek word ergazomai which means to work or to labor.
    a. Preaching the gospel is work, very hard work in the Spirit-**1 Cor 4:11-13, 2 Cor 11:27, etc.**
    b. Preaching the gospel is a spiritual undertaking-**1 Cor 9:11**
2. The words holy things, in the reference above, is from the Greek word hieros and it means priest, sacred (holy), and temple.
    a. Preaching the gospel is considered a "sacred," "priest" function in the order of Melchizedek, and a "temple" function (functioning within the spiritual temple of God's people)
    b. The scriptures are considered "priest" writings-**2 Tim 3:15**

3. Live in the reference above is translated from the Greek word esthio; and it means to eat.
   a. Thos who worked with the holy things in the temple of the Old Covenant were to "eat" from the very sacrifices the people offered to God.
   b. Ministers of the gospel should be "fed" (provide for) by the people (the temple of God) they are serving-**Gal 6:6-8**
4. Temple is the Greek word "hieros" and means priest, sacred (holy), temple.
   a. In the Old Covenant the priests ministered in the temple built by man's hand
   b. In the New Covenant of the Melchizedek order, the priests of God minister to the temple of believers-**1 Cor 3:15**
5. The word "wait" in the reference above means to be beside-present, or to attend upon.
   a. In the Old Covenant priest waited upon or served at the altars Moses and Solomon commissioned.
   b. In the New Covenant the Melchizedek priest wait upon God's "Altar," which is personified by the Lord Jesus-**Heb 13:10-13**
   c. Preaching the gospel of Jesus is considered waiting on God's Altar
6. Altar is defined as a sacrifice-place.
   a. In the Old Covenant there were literal altars Moses and Solomon built.
      i. The Brass Altar
      ii. The Altar of Incense
   b. In the New Covenant God's "Altar" is personified in the Lord Jesus Christ-**Heb 13:10-13**

c. In the New Covenant the Altar of the Lord is considered as taking communion at the Lord's Table-**1 Cor 10:18-21**

7. The word partakes is from a Greek compound word meaning to portion share together, or to share a portion together.

    a. The priests in the Old Covenant "shared" "together" with the Lord's portions given by the people.

    b. In other words, the sacrifices the people offered to God both temporarily cleanse their flesh from sins (through the blood) and sustained the priests (through the meat of the sacrifices) who worked in God's temple in things pertaining to God.

8. Ordained means to through-arrange or thoroughly arrange.

    a. The Lord has now "arranged" that as the "priests" who served the "temple" "lived" off the offerings of the people, so those who preach the gospel is to be sustained by people who are being taught-**Gal 6:6**

Titus 2:3-5-Women Priests

[3]The **aged women** likewise, that they be in behavior as **'priest-fitting,'** not **false accusers**, **not given to much wine, teachers of good things;** [4]That they may **teach** the young women to be sober, to **'befriend'** their husbands, to **'befriend'** their children, [5]To be **discreet, chaste, keepers at home, good, obedient** to their own husbands, **that the word of God be not blasphemed.**

1. The words aged women is translated from the Greek word "presbutis," transliterated as "presbytess," a senior or mature lady.

a. Presbutis is the feminine noun of the masculine noun for elders (presbytery)-**Titus 1:5, Titus 2:1, 1 Peter 5:1**
b. A woman can be "elderess"[19] in the Church just as men can be "elders."
    i. **Note:** In **1 Timothy 5:2,** the Greek word for "elder women" is (presbyteras, "eldress") is the feminine version that is used of "elders" that is used for the twenty-four elders (presbuteros) in **Revelation 4:4,** with an understanding that twenty-four (24) is a number that is symbolic of the twenty-four (24) divisions of the courses of the offices of the priesthood-**1 Chron 24, 1 Chron 25, 1 Chron 26**
    ii. Sonship is neither male nor female in Christ-**Gal 3:26-28**
        1. Thus, can women teach men? It depends! That is, I will parse the response to this question relative to a public and private behavior; and it is the Spirit of the Lord Jesus who has the final say.
        2. A mature woman can sometimes take the lead in teaching a man in conjunction with her husband (if married). In **Acts 18:26,** the oldest Greek texts have Pricila, the wife of Aquila, taking the lead in teaching Apollos the more exact way of the Lord Jesus. That is, her name was listed first of the two as they instructed Apollos.
        3. With respect to the Church in their home, Aquila is listed first; meaning he is the lead

---

[19] "Elderess" is a word I coined based on the Greek word "presbutis" (presbytess). That is, as there is a "prophetess" for the masculine "prophet," there can be "elderess" or "presbytess"

pastor/teacher for the Church they shepherd-**1 Cor 16:19, 1 Cor 11:3**

4. After the resurrection of the Lord Jesus, the angel of the Lord sent women ("Mary Magdalene and the other Mary") to direct the Apostles of the Lamb to meet the Lord Jesus in Galilee were, before His death and resurrection, He had previously directed them to meet Him-**Matt 27:1-7**

5. With that said above, a wife is not to "teach" or be "self-authoritative" over her husband, especially publicly, due to the potential to be deceived by Satan and his angels-**1 Tim 2:12-14 w/1 Cor 11:10 w/1 Cor 14:34-35**

6. Debroah was a woman Judge and prophetess in Israel, during the age of the Law, who directed "men" in battle; how much more, for those baptized "in Christ," where there is neither male nor female, a mature woman can be a teacher of men-**Judges 4:4-Judges 5:1-31, Gal 3:28**

7. There was Huldah, the prophetess who spoke judgmental, predictive, and directive words to a king (a man)-**2 Kings 22:11-20**

8. Both male and female (Simeon and Anna) prophesied to the child Jesus when Mary and Joseph went into the temple to present the child Jesus to the Lord-**Luke 1:21-40**

9. Are there women apostles? If yes, based on scriptures, there would be a selective few, identified or "signified" "upon-sign(s)" of apostles-**see Rom 16:7, 2 Cor 12:12, Acts 4:33**

2. The phrase "becomes holiness" used of women is better translated as priest-fitting. The words are from a Greek compound "hieroprepés," hieros (priest) and prepo (fitting, to tower up).

   a. Thus, women are "fit" to be "priests" of the Melchizedek order where all believers are called "sons," there is neither male nor female, all are Christ-**Gal 3:26-28**

      i. "Sonship is spiritual (neither male nor female), as the Melchizedek priesthood is spiritual.

   b. Women's behavior should be "priest-fitting" according to the order of Melchizedek.

      i. "Priest-fitting behavior of not false accusers, which means women are not to be "devils," not to be "backbiters."

         1. Judas, a man, was also called a "devil"-**John 6:70-71**

   c. "Priest-fitting behavior of not given to much wine," meaning they should "not be enslaved to much wine."

      i. Drinking is not a sin, drunkenness is sin.

      ii. However, "given too much wine" can enslave a person to wine.

   d. Women should have "priest-fitting behavior by being **"teachers of good things,"** where **"teachers of good things"** is from the Greek compound "kalodidaskalos" where **kalos is defined as attractively** good and didaskalos is defined as a teacher)

      i. "Fit" women "priests" **"teachers"** under the Melchizedek's order are to teach younger women the **"attractive"** things Paul listed.

         1. The "attractiveness" of being "pure."

         2. The "attractiveness" wives befriending their husbands.

3. The "attractiveness of wives befriending their children.

4. The "attractiveness" of wives walking in a "safe (saved)-disposition."

5. The "attractiveness" of wives being workers at home.

6. The "attractiveness" of wives being intrinsically good.

7. The "attractiveness" of wives submitted to their own husbands that the Word of God be not blasphemed.

e. "Priest-fitting behavior of **teaching**," where **"teaching"** is the Greek compound "sóphronizó;" "sozo" (saved, safe) and "phren" (disposition, both visceral and cognitive)

i. "Fit" women "priests" teaching younger women to have a "safe-disposition" according to the order of Melchizedek.

1. "Mothers" in the Lord, teaching the younger wives to feel safe both cognitively and visceral; i.e., encouraging the younger wives to feel safe befriending their husbands and children, to feel safe working at home, being good natured, feeling safe submitting to their own husbands that the Word of God be not blasphemed

Note: the term "fitting" or "towering up" is also used of the Lord Jesus' High Priesthood-**Heb 7:26.** Thus, women are also like their Lord as Paul indicated.

1 Peter 2:2-9-Holy and Royal Priesthood

[2]As newborn babies, desire the sincere milk of the word, that you may grow thereby: [3]If so be you have tasted that the Lord is gracious. [4]To whom coming, as unto a **Living Stone, 'rejected'** indeed of men, but **chosen** of God, and **precious,** [5]You also, as **living stones,** are built up a **spiritual house,** a **holy priesthood**, to **offer up spiritual sacrifices,** acceptable to God by Jesus Christ .... [9]But you are a chosen generation, **a royal priesthood ....**

1. The Lord is the Living Stone, the Chief Corner Stone who was cut out for use without man's hand to build His spiritual house of His holy priesthood and His royal priesthood-**Dan 2:34-35, Dan 2:44-45**.
2. The living stones are the people who accepts the Lord Jesus as chosen and valuable and thus, became some of the stones used for building his spiritual house for His eventual permanent habitation through the Spirit-**Eph 2:19-22**
3. The spiritual house is God's house made up of living stones people who accepts the Lord Jesus Christ. It is a building not made with man's hands-**Matt 16:17-18, Acts 17:24, Col 2:10-15, Dan 2:34-35; 44-45,**
4. The Holy priesthood is the Melchizedek priesthood of believer who are made "holy" because through "belief" they "value" the Lord Jesus as God's "chosen."
5. Offering up spiritual sacrifices is briefly listed below.
    a. Sacrifices of a broken spirit and a broken and crushed heart-**Psalm 51:17, compare Matt 11:29**
    b. Spiritual sacrifice of giving to one's apostle-**Phil 4:15-19**
    c. Presenting our bodies as living sacrifice-**Rom 12:1**
    d. Good-doing and fellowshipping-Heb 13:16

    e. Evening sacrifice of lifting hands to God-**Psalm 141:2**

    f. Sacrifice of faith-**Phil 2:17**

    g. Sacrifices of praises-**Heb 13:15**

        i. The fruit of our lips confessing His name.

6. The Lord Jesus' royal priesthood represents "kingly priests" of God according to the order of Melchizedek, our "King Jesus," our High Priest Jesus, our King of righteousness, our King of peace, our King of joy, the Lord Jesus, the King-Priest of the Highest-**Heb 7**

MELCHIZEDEK, AN UNVEILING OF JESUS

Interpretation-Types Related to Melchizedek

In this section, the intent is to unveil **some** scriptural examples of the Lord Jesus and His Church functioning according to the order of Melchizedek in the book of "The Revelation of Jesus Christ." Remember, according to the writings in the book of Hebrews and other writings of apostles Paul, Peter and John, all of the "patterns" in the Old Testament related to the Tabernacle Moses built and/or the associated Aaronic priesthood were "types" of God's "Temple," both His heavenly Temple and the Temple of the Corporate Body, His Church on earth, with the Lord Jesus being the High Priest over God's Temple according to the order of Melchizedek **(Heb 3:1-6, Heb 9, Heb 9, 1 Cor 3:16, Eph 2:21-22, 1 Pet 2:5-9, Rev 1:1 thru Rev 22:21).** This "unveiling" of Jesus Christ and His Body of believers functioning in the Melchizedek order is one of the mysteries of God concerning Jesus, the Christ that is being revealed.

This revelation ("unveiling") of the "mystery of Christ" according to the Melchizedek order started some two thousand years ago with the Lord Jesus Christ, all His apostles of the Lamb, the apostles of Christ and the writer of the book of Hebrews. This mystery of the Melchizedek order of the tribe of Judah was hidden in God from Moses; however, the mystery of Christ, our Melchizedek High-Priest, is now revealed by the Spirit of Jesus Christ. Part of the mystery of the Melchizedek order is concerning the spiritual "priest-togetherness" of Jesus, the Christ, "together" "with" His "royal priesthood," again, functioning according to the order of Melchizedek. Saying it another way, the Book of the Revelation of Jesus Christ also consists of the "unveiling" of the Lord Jesus, as the High-Priest, according to the order of Melchizedek, and the revealing of His royal priesthood also functioning as priests of God "executing His verdicts written."

Hebrews 8:1-The Lord's Right Hand

Now of the things which we have spoken this is the **'Head:'** We have such a **High-Priest**, who is **seated in the right hand of the throne** of the **'Great-togetherness'** in the heavens.

Psalm 110:1-2; 4-6: [1]The Lord said to **my Lord,** "Sit at **My right hand,** till I make **Your enemies** Your footstool." [2]The Lord shall send the rod of Your strength out of Zion. **Rule** in the midst of Your **enemies!** .... [4]The Lord has **sworn** and will not relent, **"You are a priest forever according to the order of Melchizedek."** [5]**The Lord** is at Your **right hand; He shall execute kings in the day of His wrath.** [6]He shall **judge** among the **nations, He shall fill the places with dead bodies,** He shall **execute** the heads of many countries.

Psalms 149:5-9: [5]Let **the saints (lit., kind ones)** be joyful in glory; let them sing aloud on their beds. [6]Let the high praises of God be in their mouth, and a two-edged sword in their hand, [7]to **execute vengeance on the nations,** and punishments on the peoples; [8]to bind their kings with chains, and their nobles with fetters of iron; [9]**to execute on them the written judgment**—this honor have all His **saints (lit., kind ones).**

The Lord Jesus, in **Luke 20:41-44**, made it clear that what king David said in **Psalm 110** is referencing the Lord Jesus as both "Son" of David and "Lord" of David, the Lordship of Jesus' eternal Melchizedek priesthood according to God's "oath." This "oath" is related to the resurrection of Jesus

Christ, who is now seated in God's Throne as our High-Priest. In addition, we have learned in the section expounding on **Hebrews 8:1-5** that the Lord Jesus, as our High Priest according to the order of Melchizedek is "in the right hand of the Throne of the 'Great-togetherness' in the Heavens," as David prophesied of the Lord Jesus in **Psalm 110:1 and Psalm 110:5.** David said in **Psalm 110,** it is from the "right hand" of God Jesus' Melchizedek order would administer judgments to the Lord's enemies. "The Lord has **sworn** and will not relent, "You are a **priest forever according to the order of Melchizedek."** The **Lord is at Your right hand;** He shall **execute kings** in the day of His wrath **(Psalm 110:4-5).**

Thus, there is a "course" of mature priests of the Melchizedek order who obeys the direction of the Lord, their High-Priest, relative to executing judgments and justice. That is, counterintuitively, it is the priesthood of "saints" (the "kind ones") who will execute severity of the "judgments written." They will do this by the commandments of the living God, the living Lamb of God and the Seven Spirits of God. That is, it is only those whom God have matured in love (kindness and longsuffering) who will be chosen, being part of Jesus' "priest-togetherness," to display the severity of God because severity is not the first option in their new nature.

Therefore, as the Melchizedek order shows the "kindness of God" to those who by faith accepts the sacrifices of Jesus, the blood of Jesus, the death, burial and resurrection of Jesus Christ, so the "severity" of God will also be administered against the enemies of God through the Melchizedek order, as depicted in the Book of the Revelation of Jesus Christ. The same God who shows kindness to those of faith is the same God who shows severity to those who reject Jesus **(Romans 11:22).** The Lamb of God who was slain for our sins is the same Lamb who will exhibit "wrath" **(Rev 5:6, Rev 5:9, Rev 6:12).** The same priestly vessels that are used to sanctify God's people are some of the same priestly vessels that will release God's severity, at God's command. For example, the Altar of Incense that represents the incense of prayer in conjunction with the fumigated incense that protects the high priests from death, is the same Altar of Incense that is used to release the plagues of the Sixth Trumpet that causes death **(Leviticus 16, Revelation 8, Revelation 9, etc.).** Thus, any severity of wrath from the living God is always tempered with His mercy, tempered with the intercession of the Lord Jesus, the Lamb's nature, and so forth. With all that said, lets us briefly look at a few scriptures of the Revelation of Jesus Christ that can signify the workings of the more excellent ministry of the Melchizedek order.

Revelation 1:5-Sin-free Priesthood

… Jesus Christ, the faithful witness, the firstborn from the dead, and the ruler of the kings of the earth. To Him who loves us and has **released us from our sins by His blood.**

1. The application of blood for the atonement of sins is a High Priest function-**Lev 16**
2. This verse above demonstrates the Lord Jesus, our High-Priest, functioning according to the order Melchizedek eternally **releasing** us from sins through His blood-**Heb 9:11-15**
   a. The Lord Jesus is the only Man to live sinless. Jesus had **no** sin, and He did **no** sin-**Heb 4:15, Heb 9:28, Heb 9:14, 1 Peter 1:19, John 8:46.**

    b. Bing under Jesus "grace" through His blood applied to our hearts or consciences, we are "freed from sins," making us "sin-free"-**Rom 6:14-18, Rom 6:22, John 1:29, Rev 1:5, etc.**

Revelation 1:6- Kingdom of Priests

Who has made us to be a **kingdom, priests to His God** and **Father**—to Him be the glory and power forever and ever! Amen.

1. The beloved apostle John made it clear in the reference above that "us" [the seven-fold Churches (then and now) of Jesus Christ] are royal priests to Jesus' God-**1 Pet 2:9**

2. The beloved apostle John made it clear in the reference above that "us" (the seven-fold Churches (then and now) of Jesus Christ) are a "kingdom" of "priests," which according to the book of Hebrews are the Melchizedek's priesthood-**1 Pet 2:9**

3. The heavenly Father have always wanted a "kingdom of priests," in the priesthood of Jesus-**Exodus 19:6, Col 1:13**

Revelation 1:12; 1:20-The Seven Lampstands

[12]Then I turned to see the voice that was speaking with me. And having turned, I saw **seven golden lampstands** .... [20]This is the mystery of the seven stars you saw in My right hand and of the **seven golden lampstands:** The seven stars are the angels of the seven churches, and **the seven lampstands** are **the seven churches.**

1. The Lampstand was a vessel or furniture of the Tabernacle God asked Moses to build according to the pattern he saw in heaven-**Ex 25:31-40**

2. The Lampstand is only administered to by the High Priests-**Ex 30:7-8**

    a. The High Priest trimmed the lamps of the lampstand and supplied the oil to the lampstand-**i.e., Ex 30:8**

3. The seven Lampstands represents the seven Churches.

    a. Thus, one (1) lampstand equals one (1) Church for a total of seven (7) Lampstands and **not** one (1) lampstand equaling seven (7) Churches or the seven-fold Churches of Jesus, the Christ

        i. In every age there exist all seven types of the Churches the Lord addressed in **Revelation 2** and **Revelation 3;** and all of Jesus' seven Churches in the earth functions in the fruit and gifts of the Spirit depicted on the Lampstand, at a minimum, in the nine fruit of the Spirit, and at least nine gifts of the Spirit, of the twenty-two gifts listed in the Bible-**Gal 5:22-25, 1 Cor 12:1-31, Rom 12:3-8, 1 Peter 4:11, w/Ex 25:31-40**

    b. The seven Churches functioning as seven Lampstands are located in the holy place of the Tabernacle related to the Churches of God and His priesthood functioning in the order of Melchizedek.

    c. **Note:** As Jesus' Churches function as seven lampstands and the table of showbread (the table of the bread of purpose) for the last 2000 years, the Church is to transition and function from God's Throne, from the Holy of Holies, according to the order of Melchizedek, according to all the furniture in the Holy of Holies, just before the millennium rule and during the millennium rule of Christ with his resurrected priesthood-**Heb 9:2-5, Rev 4, Rev 11, Rev 20**

Revelation 1:13-Jesus' Priestly Clothing

And **among the lampstands** was One like **the Son of Man,** dressed in **a long robe,** with a **golden sash around His chest.**

1. One like the Son of Man, the Lord Jesus, among (or literally, "in the middle") of all seven Lampstands demonstrates the Lord Jesus as the Melchizedek High Priest who internally trims (attend to) the lights of the lampstands (Churches) as Aaron was instructed to do for the lampstand in the Tent of Witness-**Ex 30:8**
2. The clothing to Jesus' feet and the golden sash around His chest can be representative of His Melchizedek's High Priest governmental clothing and also His High Priest "strength" seen in the sash, and so on-**Isaiah 22:21, Ex 28:4; 28:31.**

Revelation 4:4-The 24 Courses

Surrounding the throne were twenty-four other thrones, and on these thrones sat **twenty-four elders** dressed in white, with **golden crowns** on their heads.

1. As a reminder, Melchizedek was made like Jesus, our Righteous King, Jesus our High-Priest-**Matt 2:2, John 18:37, Heb 3:1, Heb 5, etc.**
2. Melchizedek kingly priesthood (priest-togetherness) equals God's Royal Priesthood, Holy Priesthood who are "together" "with" the Lord Jesus's High priesthood-**Heb 7:11; 7:12; 7:24, 1 Pet 2:9, 1 Pet 2:6**
3. Melchizedek kingly priesthood also is represented by Jesus' twenty-four (24) Elders of kings-priests-**Rev 4:4**
   a. Twenty-four (24) equals twenty-four divisions of the courses of the high priesthood-**1 Chronicles 24**

    i. The high priests minister to God in things pertaining to God in the Holy Places-**Luke 1:5-10, Ex 30:6-8, Lev 16, etc.**

b. There are to be Melchizedek's priesthood divisions (representative of twenty-four (24)) of prophetic priest psalmists-**1 Chron 25**

    i. They were also "princes" in the "warfare" of God's "host" of the "army" who warred **prophetically** through music and worship-**1 Chron 25:1**

        i. A couple of expressions of the priesthood of the twenty-four (24) Elders is ministering to the Lord "in things pertaining to God;" such as, **"worshipping"** God and the **"singing"** of a **"new song"** (spontaneous prophetic song) to the Lamb of God-**Rev 4:10, Rev 5:8-9 w/Col 3:16 w/Psalm 96:1, w/Rev 14:1-3, Rev 5:14, Rev 11:16**

    ii. The also ministered with harps, cymbals which represents being baptized in the Holy Spirit and singing in the gift tongues "in love" with their spirits and in the Spirit-**1 Chron 25:1-3 w/1 Cor 13:1 w/1 Cor 14:14-15**

c. There are to be Melchizedek's priesthood divisions (representative of twenty-four (24)) of gatekeepers who" serves in the House of God" **(1 Chron 26)**

    i. The gatekeepers are priests who watch and discern who genuinely or disingenuously enters the Body of Christ to either accept or give warning-**Acts 5:12-15, Rev 21:12, Rev 21:27, Rev 22:14**

d. There are to be Melchizedek's priesthood divisions (representative of twenty-four (24)) of the captains who "minister to the King (Jesus) in any 'word of the courses"-**1 Chron 27**

   i.   These appear to be traveling ministers because they came in and went out monthly -**1 Chron 27:1**

e. The twenty-four courses of the high priests all have certain days of servicing the holy palaces according to their "course"-**Luke 1:5-10**

f. Therefore, twenty-four (24) is also symbolic of King Jesus Kingdom of priests, in general.

g. These examples of twenty-four (24) courses of multiple functions shows Jesus our High Priest requirement for His royal priesthood to share the responsibilities in the courses (work) of the Melchizedek order-**Eph 4:15-16, 1 Cor 14:26-33, Rev 16:1-12, Heb 5:7, etc.**

h. The twenty-four (24) Elders sat on thrones (seats) with victor's crowns.

   i.   Therefore, like their King Jesus, they are also "crowned" in the service of God's priesthood through conquering their spiritual enemies so their foes cannot prevent them from executing Jesus' priesthood in heaven or on earth -**2 Tim 4:8, Rev 12:12**

d. The twenty-four (24) Elders equals "matured men with seasoned judgment," "Seniors," therefore matured, older men, **ambassadors,** presbytery of the living God **(2 Cor 5:20,** see also Strong's #4245, #4244, #4243, BibleHub.com)

   i.   Thus, the twenty-four (24) Elders with twenty-four (24) crowns and twenty-four (24) seats equal the "matured" Melchizedek **kingly priesthood** of Jesus Christ-**1 Pet 2:9, Rev 4:4, Rev 20-4-6.**

ii. See **Heb 7:11; 7:12; 7:24** where "priesthood" is literally "priest togetherness (hieros (priest) and sun (together, with).

1. That is, we are priests together with our High-Priest, Jesus Christ!

Revelation 5:6-The Slain Lamb

Then I saw a **Lamb who appeared to have been slain, standing in the center of the throne,** encircled by the **four living creatures** and the elders. The Lamb had seven horns and seven eyes, which represent the seven Spirits of God sent out into all the earth.

1. The Lamb having been slain represents the Lord Jesus as the "freshly slain sacrifice" **(Heb 10:20)** which is related to the Brass Altar where the sacrifices were offered-**Ex 38:30**
2. The four living creatures operates in the "temple" where the Lord's Throne is; and is therefore, an example that shows the truth of ministry related to the Lamb's Melchizedek priesthood in the "tabernacle in heaven"-**Isaiah 6:1-3, Heb 8, Heb 9**
3. God's Throne is "the Throne of Grace," is "the Ark of the Covenant" where God "reigns ... dwelling between the cherubs"-**Heb 4:14-16 w/Num 7:89 w/Psalm 99:1**
    i. Therefore, the slain Lamb in the Throne is the Lord Jesus in the middle of the Mercy Seat, the Throne of Grace administering His love.

Revelation 5:8-10-Priests to Reign

[8]When He had taken the scroll; the four living creatures and the twenty-four elders fell down before the Lamb. Each one had a harp, and they were holding golden bowls full of incense, which are the prayers of the saints. [9]And they sang a new song: "Worthy are You to take the scroll and open its

seals, because You were slain, and **by Your blood** You purchased for God **those from every tribe and tongue and people** and nation. [10]**You have made them** to be **a kingdom** and **priests** to **serve our God**, and **they will reign upon the earth."**

1. Jesus, being the **"slain"** Lamb, by **His blood "purchased** for God those from every tribe and tongue and people and nation."
   a. Jesus' "better blood" redeemed and purchases mankind from all peoples-**Heb 12:24 w/Rev 5:9**
   b. The Melchizedek kingdom and priesthood, through the blood of Jesus, is inclusive of all peoples. It is not an exclusive order consisting only of a certain race or people.
      i. In the Melchizedek order, there is redemptive **equality**-**Rom 10:12, Rom 3:22**
         1. All the "stadiums" of measures in the New Jerusalem (New Priest-Peace) are **"equal"**-**Rev 21:16**
2. God made His purchased **"people"** a **"kingdom,"** not just a kingdom emphasizing land masses-**1 Pet 2:5, 1 Pet 2:9**
   a. God's kingdom is a kingdom of priests, as was His intent from Moses' days-**Ex 19:6**
3. Jesus Melchizedek priests consist of His redeemed mankind "from every tribe and tongue and people and nation."
4. The priesthood of God, according to the order of Melchizedek will **"reign upon the earth"**-see also **Rev 20:1-6, 1 Cor 4:8**

Revelation 6:9-The Fifth Seal and the Altar

And when the **Lamb** opened the **fifth seal,** I saw under the **altar** the **souls** of those **who had been slain** for the word of God and for the testimony they had upheld.

1. The Lamb, the Lord Jesus, opening the Fifth Seal demonstrate that the seals are also a High Priest function related to the "slain Lamb" according to the order of Melchizedek.
   a. In other words, it is only "the Lion of the tribe of Judah," the tribe of the Melchizedek who is worthy to open the seals, through His Lamb's nature, as the High-Priest-**Rev 5:5 w/Heb 7:14-15**
2. The "Altar" in heaven is also a temple function and a "priesthood" function according to the order of Melchizedek.
3. The souls under the Altar can be representative of those who sacrificed their bodies as living sacrifices to God, sacrificing being a priesthood function-**Rom 12:1, Phil 2:17, 2 Tim 4:6**

Revelation 8:1-2-The Seven Trumpets

[1]When the Lamb opened the seventh seal; there was silence in heaven for about **half an hour.** [2]And I saw the **seven angels** who stand before God, and they were given **seven trumpets.**

1. Half an hour may represent the following:
   a. A literal ½ hour in heaven
   b. Or based on "one day with God is as a thousand years," it may be symbolic of ~21 years (1,000 years/24 hours = 41.67 years/hour; hence a ½ of hour is ~42/2 = ~21 years-**2 Pet 3:8**
   c. Or it may be based on a year equaling a day; and thus, symbolic of one-half of a full prophetic week of years

(360/24 hours) = 15 years/hour; 15 years = 1 hour; hence ½ hour = 7.5 years or 7 years depending on the true Hebrew calendar year based on 7 days/week)-**Num 14:34**

2. The Seven angels with the seven trumpets are priests' function-**Joshua 6:4**

3. The seven trumpets can also represent the seven-fold Melchizedek priesthood judging the world through the sounding of the seven trumpets (God's priests-prophets), the world being typified as "Jericho"—fragrance of the moon.

4. The "moon" is symbolic of the "lesser light" ruling over the night (the authority of darkness)-**Gen 1:16**

   a. Hence, as God judge the wall of Jericho and Jericho through the seven priests with the seven trumpets, so the world who are under the authority of darkness will be judge through the seven angels (Melchizedek priesthood) with the seven trumpets (God's mature prophets and apostles)

   b. **Note:** Ezekiel was a priest-prophet-**Ezekiel 1:3 w/Ezekiel 2:1-5, etc.**

   c. Trumpets represent prophets and watchmen-**Ezekiel 33:1-7**

   d. Apostles also do the same as prophets in a greater capacity-**Jude 1:17, 2 Pet 3:2**

      i. In **Jude 1:17 and 2 Pet 3:2,** we see that apostles also prophesy, as the prophets, also prophesy; however, apostles also give "commands" (lit., "in-limits"), a facet of the greater authority of apostles is also documented in **2 Pet 3:2**

Revelation 8:3-4-The Gold Altar of Incense
[3]Then another angel, who had a **golden censer,** came and stood at the **altar.** He was given much **incense to offer,** along with the prayers of all the saints, on the **golden altar** before the throne. [4]And the **smoke of the incense,** together with the prayers of the saints, rose up before God from the hand of the angel.

1. The gold censer, the gold altar, and the offering of the incense is a function of the High-Priest-**Lev 16**
    a. Therefore, this event that happened before the seven priests-angels trumpeted is a function of Jesus our High Priest according to the order of Melchizedek and His priesthood of believers offering up incense (prayers)-**Psalm 141:2, Rev 5:8**
    b. Also, as the incense of fumigated fire protected the high priest from death, so the fumigation of the gold frankincense of the "prayers of all saints" will protects God's Melchizedek priests from death during the judgments of the seven trumpets-**Lev 16:12-23 w/Rev 8:5-7**
        i. This is an example of God's goodness to His believers and God's severity to those who reject Jesus (Jews and Gentiles alike)-**Rom 11:22, Rev 9:4-6**

Revelation 9:13-14-The Four Horns
[13]Then the **sixth angel sounded his trumpet,** and I heard a voice from the **four horns of the golden altar** before God [14]saying to the sixth angel with the trumpet, "Release the four angels who are bound at the great river Euphrates.

1. Remember the seven angels with the seven trumpets is a priest function-**Joshua 6:4**

2. The Gold Altar is also temple furniture and administered to by the High-Priest-**Lev 16**
3. This judgment directed by the four horns of the Gold Altar is judgment according to the order of Melchizedek related to wrath-**Psalm 110, Rev 6:16-17**
   a. The horns of the Gold Altar were atoned with blood once a year-**Lev 16**
   b. Blood has a voice (forgiveness or vengeance)-**Heb 12:24, Gen 4:10**
      i. This plague release by the "voice" of the four horns of the Gold Altar is a direct result of a lack of repentance and rejection of Jesus better atoning blood.

Revelation 11:1-Apostolic Measuring

[1]Then I was given a measuring **rod** like a staff and was told, "Go and **measure** the **temple of God** and the **altar,** and count the number of **worshipers** there.

1. In this example above, an apostolic priest (the apostle John who Jesus loved) is authorized to measure[20] the "temple of God"-**1 Cor 3:17**
   a. Temple of God is God's body of believers who "house" the Holy Spirit-**1 Cor 3:17, 2 Cor 6:16**
   b. Those "worshippers" who are in the "measure" of the Temple of God will be protected from the nations trampling them-**Rev 11:2**
2. Also, in the reference above, apostolic Melchizedek priesthood is authorized to measure the "altar."

---

[20] You may refer to my book *Ezekiel-the House-the City-the Land (Interpreting the Patterns)* for an extensive exegete on measuring or the measure of Christ

a. Altar represents sacrifice place (spiritual sacrifices)-**1 Pet 2**

b. Altar represents preachers of the gospel-**1 Cor 9:13-14**

c. Altar represents place of the sacrifice of prayer according to the order of Melchizedek- **Heb 5:6-7, Rev 8, Ps 141:2**

d. **Note:** the use of the word **"rod"** shows that the beloved John apostolic measuring is not only "in love" (as we think love to be) or only in "the spirit of mildness"-**1 Cor 4:21**

   i. Remember the same God that is "good" can also be "severe"-**Rom 11:22**

e. Those "worshippers" who are in the "measure" of the "Altar" will be protected from the nations trampling them-**Rev 11:2**

Revelation 15:2-The Sea of Glass

²And I saw something like a **sea of glass mixed with fire**, beside which stood **those** who had **conquered** the beast and its image and the number of its name ....

1. Sea of glass is a literal sea of glass like "crystal" which is before God's throne-**Rev 4:6**

2. Sea of Glass mixed with fire is symbolized by the "molten (hard, fused) sea" Solomon built-**2 Chro 4:2, Jer 27:19**

   a. "Molten" is translated as "hard" in **Job 38:38**

   b. "Hardness" coincides with the crystalized sea-**Rev 4:6**

   c. Molen means poured melted and fiery metal.

   d. Molten sea is symbolic of the hard-fiery sea of glass.

3. Standing on the sea of glass mixed with fire equals baptism in fire (testing by fiery trials, tried by fire)-**1 Cor 10:2, Mat 3:11, 1 Pet 1:7, 1 Cor 3:12-13**

a. Jesus baptizes us with the Holy Spirit and fire **(Matt 3:11)**; all were baptized unto Moses in the sea **(I Cor 10:2, Exodus 15)**; believers will be baptized unto Jesus in the sea of glass mixed with fire **(Matt 3:11)**

b. **God is a consuming fire (Heb 12:29).**

c. **The glorified Lord Jesus is fire from His waist going up and fire from His waist going down (Ezekiel 1:27; 8:2)**

4. The sea of glass mixed with fire, prefigured by the molten-hard sea, is for **"priests to wash"** themselves-2 **Chron 4:6**

   a. **Note:** The Molten Sea built for the priesthood related to the temple Solomon built is prefigured by the "Brass Laver" Moses commissioned, which was made of "looking glass" for washing the priest; and it is like a mirror reflecting one's true self-**Ex 30:18, Ex 38:8, Ex 40:30, 2 Cor 3:18, James 1:23-25**

      i. The Lord's Church is now "washed with the water of [God's] Word"-**Eph 5:26**

   b. The "those" in **Rev 15:2** are "those" who were once not a people of God but overcame the beast, its image and its number to become "priests unto God" through the "manifestation" of the Lord's "righteous acts"-**Rev 15:1-2 w/Rev 15:4 w/1 Peter 2:9-10 w/2 Chron 4:6 w/Rev 5:10 w/Rev 20:4-6**

   c. **Note:** The same "red sea" (lit., "termination sea," or "sea of termination") into which the Israelites were baptized unto Moses was the same "sea" that "terminated" their persecutors, the Egyptians-**Ex 14, 1 Cor 10:2.** In like manner, the same sea of glass mixed with fire that washes the overcoming priests, is the same sea of fire that helped them to overcome (burn off) the influences of the beast as depicted in **Rev 13 w/Rev 17 w/Rev 15:1-4**

       i. In other words, baptisms (Holy Spirit baptism, water baptism, fire baptism, baptism into the cup of suffering) in/through the Lord Jesus Christ, terminates any past sins, any past enemies, and so on that may be pursuing a believer.

5. **Note:** Here is some "strong meat" for Jesus' matured priesthood. According to the Hebrew reading in **2 Chronicles 4:5**, complete "conquest" (overcoming) occurred when the "molten-hard sea" is filled to three thousand baths (3000 years) from Christ's resurrection.

   a. The three thousand (3000) baths may prophetically, equals three thousand (3000) years, which shows the work of the Lord Jesus' priesthood continuing beyond the current Church age of 2000 years or so, into the Sabbath Millennium -**see Rev 20:1-6** and the exegete for **Rev 20:6** in this section

      i. The scriptures document the molten sea being filled at 2000 baths and 3000 baths-**2 Chron 4:5, 1 Kings 7:26**

      ii. This may also mean that in addition to the sea of glass mingled with fire purging people from beast, its image and its number, at some time before the Lord Jesus descends from heaven to defeat the beast, it may take an entire millennium [the Sabbath Millennium (3000-2000 = 1000)] to purge from the earth the lingering influence from the three beasts (Satan, the Beast, the False Prophet)-**Rev 19:20-20:1-3**

Revelation 15:5-7-The Seven Prophet-Priests

[5]After this I looked, and the **temple—**the **tabernacle of the Testimony—**was opened **in heaven.** [6]And **out of the temple**

came the **seven angels** with **the seven plagues**, dressed in clean and bright linen, and girded with golden sashes around their chests. [7]Then one of the four living creatures gave the seven angels seven golden bowls full of the wrath of God, who lives forever and ever. [8]And the temple was filled with smoke from the glory of God and from His power; and no one could enter **the temple** until the seven plagues of the seven angels were completed.

1. The temple, the Tabernacle of the Testimony is the tabernacle in heaven according to the order of Melchizedek-**Heb 8, Heb 9, Heb 7, Heb 6, Heb 5**
2. Seven angels represent seven priests (priests are called angels)-**Malachi 2:7**
3. The seven angels came **out of the temple** in heaven is a function of the Melchizedek's high priesthood migrating between heaven and earth-**Rev 15:5-7 w/ Rev 16:1**
   a. In the book of Hebrews, we learn that the "people" of God can now function as high priests entering the Holy Places, themselves, with and through the better blood of the Lord Jesus-**Heb 9:7-9 w/Heb 10:19-20**
      i. The Old Covenant only allowed the High-Priest, with the blood of animals, into "the Second" of the two Holy Places (the Holy of Holies)-**Heb 9:7-9**
      ii. In the New Covenant of the Melchizedek order, the Lord Jesus our High Priest also entered into "the Second" of the two "Holy Places" with His own "better blood;" and we now also as a corporate high priests of the Melchizedek order can also enter behind the Veil through the same better blood of our Lord Jesus applied to our conscience-**Heb 9:7-8 w/Heb 10:19-22**

4. The seven angels are seven "Zadok" (righteous) priests of Jesus' Melchizedek order-**Ezekiel 44, Mal 2:7**
   a. Linen represents righteous acts-**Rev 19:8 w/Rev 15:4 w/Ex 39:27**
5. The seven angels are seven prophets-**Rev 17:1 w/Rev 19:9-10 w/Rev 21:15 w/Rev 22:8-9**
6. The seven angels are seven fellow servants of John-**Rev 17:1 w/Rev 19:9-10 w/Rev 21:15 w/Rev 22:8-9**
7. The seven angels are the prophet-priest ministry of Jesus' Melchizedek order and His priests administering the seven last plages of God's "hot-anger"-**Rev 15:6**

Revelation 19:11-16-Jesus' Many Crowns

[11]Then I saw heaven standing open, and there before me was a white horse. And its rider is called Faithful and True. With **righteousness** He judges and wages **war.** [12]He has eyes like blazing fire, and **many royal crowns** on His head. He has a name written on Him that only He Himself knows. [13]He is dressed in a **robe dipped in blood,** and His **Name** is The **Word of God.** [14]The armies of heaven, dressed in fine **linen,** white and pure, follow Him on white horses. [15]And from His mouth proceeds a sharp sword with which to strike down the nations, and He will rule them with an iron scepter. He treads the winepress of the fury of the wrath of God the Almighty. [16]And He has a name written on His robe and on His thigh: **KING** OF KINGS AND **LORD** OF LORDS.

6. "Many royal crowns" include, but not limited to, the Kingship of His Melchizedek order.
   a. Melchizedek is a compound word Melek (King) and Zadok (Righteous One)-**Heb 7**
      i. King Jesus' judges and makes war "with righteousness." It follows that when God's royal

priests live "righteously" "together" with the "Righteous One," Jesus our Melchizedek, war and judgment is automatically made against our enemies.

7. Robe dipped in blood means as the high priests of the Old Covenant was sprinkled with blood, so Jesus our High Priest according to the order of Melchizedek rides with a robe dipped (or baptized) in blood-**Ex 29:21**

8. Robe dipped in blood is the fulfilment of the Lord Jesus, the greater "Judah" "who washed His garments in the blood of grapes" (the wine of His blood)-**Gen 49:11, 1 Cor 11:25**

9. The Name of the Rider is the "Word of God" is the Lord Jesus, "**the Word** made flesh and 'Tabernacled" among us-**John 1:14, Heb 4:12-13**

    a. Note: no one knows the Word of God like Jesus-**Rev 19:12-13, Rev 5:1-5**

10. Armies of heaven dressed in fine linen are His armies dressed in priests' garments and His armies dressed in righteous acts-**Rev 19:8, Ex 28:38**

    a. **Note:** remember, the word "order" is a military term meaning arrangement of troops in battle formation. Hence, these armies include Jesus' Melchizedek order.

Revelation 20:6-Resurrected Priesthood

Blessed and **holy** are those who share in the **first resurrection!** The second death has no power over them, but they will be **priests of God** and of Christ, and will **reign with Him** for a **thousand** years.

1. The first resurrection is the resurrection of the holy, the blessed and the just, **"in Christ"**-1 Thes 4:16, Rev 20:6, 1 Pet 2:5, Luke 14:14, etc.

2. The first resurrection saints are "priest of God and of Christ"-**Rev 20:6**

    a. Since our Lord Jesus Christ is the High "Priest forever according to the order of Melchizedek," these resurrected "priests" are also priests according to the order of Melchizedek-**Heb 7:21-22**

    b. The resurrection Jesus' disciples will be a continuation of Jesus' Melchizedek priests "together" in eternal bodies "with" Him ruling on earth 1000 years-**Rev 5:10**

3. The first resurrection saints will be "reigning" kings with God and of Christ-**1 Pet 2:9, 1 Pet 2:5, Rev 1:6**

    a. This will also be the fulfillment of Paul's prayer concerning the saints reigning so Paul can also reign with them and Christ-**1 Cor 4:8**

    b. The "first resurrection" is the same as "the dead in Christ" who "will **rise first**" during the coming of the Lord-**1 Thess 4:15-17, Rev 20:4-6, Zach 14:1-5 w/1 Thess 3:13**

        i. The firs resurrection occurs during the "Trumpet of God, which is synonymous with the "Seventh Trumpet" and also synonymous with the "Last Trumpet."

            1. Trumpet of God means the "Trumpet of 'Theos'" which means the "Trumpet of the 'Placer'"-**1 Thes 4:16**

                a. "Theos" is defined as "Placer" and is the root word for "thithemi" (to place). God is the "Placer" of all things-**John 1:1-2, 1 Cor 12:18**

                b. In the first resurrection God, the "Placer," will **"place"** His sons and daughters ["adoption" (lit., "son-placing") fulfilled in redemption of our bodies]" as priests, rulers and shepherds of the habitable earth, placed as judges of angels, placed as judges of the habitable earth, and so on-**Rom 8:23, Eph 1:5, Gal 4:5-6, Heb 2:5-13. 1 Cor 6:2-3**

2. The Seventh Trumpet is synonymous with the last trumpet in the series of seven-**Rev 8:2 w/Rev 10:7 w/Rev 11:15-17**

   a. Note: there is no other trumpet mentioned after the Seventh Trumpet; hence the 7th Trumpet is the "Last Trumpet"

   b. The 7th Trumpet sounds for "days"-**Rev 10:7**

3. The Last Trumpet is the "The 'Eschatos' Trumpet-**1 Cor 15:51-57**

   a. "Eschatos" is defined as the "last" of a series-**Strong's #2078**

      i. Thus, the "last" trumpet of a series of seven is the Seventh Trumpet-**Rev 8:2**

   b. "Eschatos" is also defined as the "final" (the furthest extreme-end)-**Strong's #2078**

      i. Since the 7th Trumpet sounds for "days," **beginning** at **Rev 10:7, t**he first resurrection may conclude during the "furthest" of the "days" of the sounding of the 7th Trumpet-**Rev 10:6-7 w/Rev 11:7-14 w/Rev 11:15-17 w/1 Cor 15:50-52**

4. The phrase "reign with Him a thousand years" is the resurrected saints reigning a thousand years on earth with the Lord Jesus Christ void of Satan's seduction; and

after 1000 years, Satan and his angels will be cast into the Lake of Fire, the Second Death-**Rev 20:1-3, Rev 20:7-10, Matt 25:41**

a. An angel will come down from heaven at the beginning of the Millennium using a great chain to "govern" (seize and control) the dragon, the "'original' serpent" (the serpent in the garden of Eden) which is the Devil and Satan-**Rev 12:9, Rev 20:1-3, Gen 3:1, 2 Cor 11:3**

b. The angel will use the great chain to bind Satan for 1000 years-**Rev 20:1-3**

   i. The 1000-year binding is with the "great chain" not the abyss-**Rev 20:3**

      1. **Note:** it seems the angel has the power to set the duration of the binding of the chain

      2. For example, there are eternal "binding" with "eternal chains"-**Jude 1:6**

      3. There are also "chains of 'gloom'"-**2 Pet 2:4**

   ii. Satan is first "chain-bound" for 1000 years, then he was also locked up for those 1000 years.

c. The angel will cast the "bound" dragon in the abyss, lock the dragon in the abyss, and seal over the dragon so that he can no longer seduce the nations for 1000 years.

d. For 1000 years, humanity will be free of satanic seduction, during which the Christ with God's resurrected Melchizedek priests will function in the priesthood, converting the nations to priests and Levites, teaching all the nations in things pertaining to the knowledge of God; in example, teaching the nations about the Lord Jesus, coordinating the gatherings of the nations to the yearly worship (Feast of Tabernacles), or sabbatical worship of Jesus, the

King, or monthly worship of the King, Jesus, and so on-**Isaiah 66:21-23, Zach 14:1-9; w/Zach 14: 14:16-19, Mal 2:7, Rev 20:4-6, etc.**

1. The Christ "rule" or "shepherding" in the millennium will be with a "rod of iron"-**Ps 2:9, Rev 2:27. Rev 12:5, Rev 19:15**

   a. Rod signifies Jesus' shepherding of the nations will not be in the spirit of meekness towards those who resist His requirements during the millennium-**1 Cor 4:21, Zach 14:16-19**

   b. Rod of iron signifies that during Christ's millennium rule, Jesus' will be shepherding the nations with an unyielding rod of iron that will breaks all things and subdues all things-**Dan 2:40b, Zach 14:16-19**

ii. During the 1000-year reign of Christ and Melchizedek priest-togetherness with Him, the house of Satan will be spoiled as patterned in **Matthew 12:28-29**

iii. During the Sabbath Millennium, the resurrected saints and those who will be converted to Christ during the millennium will be doing similar power work as the Lord Jesus prefigured on the sabbath days when he came in the flesh ~2000 years ago-**Heb 4:9**

   1. i.e., the Lord Jesus healed on the sabbaths-Mat **12:10**

   2. i.e., the Lord Jesus taught the people on the sabbaths-**Luke 6:6**

   3. i.e., the Lord Jesus made the blind to see on the sabbath-**John 9:14**

4. The Lord Jesus made it clear that the Sabbath was made for man and not man for the sabbath-**Mark 2:27 w/Heb 2:5-10 w/Heb 4:1-10, etc.**

   a. Therefore, the Sabbath Millennium is for "man" to rule and subdue all enemies-**Rev 20:1-6, Heb 2:1-10 w/1 Cor 15:24-26, etc.**

e. After the 1000-year rule of Christ, Melchizedek King-Priest and His Melchizedek priesthood of resurrected believers, Satan will be release for a season to test the nations faithfulness to Jesus.

   i. God has so ordained that every person must be tested for genuineness in serving God freely, including our Lord Jesus-**Rev 20:7-10 w/Matt 4:1-11, Gen 21:1-19, James 1:12-15, 1 Peter 1:6-9, etc.**

   ii. After the testing of the nations, Satan will then be cast eternally into the Lake of Fire that was originally prepared for him-**Rev 20:10 w/Rev 20:14, Mat 25:41**

5. **Note:** Those, in Christ, who partake of the first resurrection will have the ability to migrate between heaven and earth to present themselves before God in heaven according to the order of Melchizedek and execute the Melchizedek priesthood on earth-**Rev 5:9-10, Luke 24:14 w/Luke 24:30-31, Mark 16:11-13, John 1:50-51, Eph 2:4-6, 2 Cor 12:1-4**

May the grace of our Lord Jesus Christ continue to be with your spirits. COME LORD JESUS! WE WELCOME YOUR COMING IN IN THE TRUMPET OF GOD!

OTHER BOOKS

Poiema, by Judith Peart
Wisdom from Above, by Judith Peart
Procreation, Understanding Sex, and Identity, by Judith Peart
100 Nevers, by Judith Peart
The Shattered and the Healing by Judith Peart
The Lamb, by Donald Peart
Jesus' Resurrection, Our Inheritance, by Donald Peart.
Sexuality, By Donald Peart
Forgiven 490 Times, by Donald Peart w/Judith Peart!
The Days of the Seventh Angel, By Donald Peart
The Torah (The Principle) of Giving, by Donald Peart
The Time Came, by Donald Peart
The Last Hour, the First Hour, the Forty-Second Generation, by Donald Peart
Vision Real, by Donald Peart
The False Prophet, Alias, Another Beast V1, by Donald Peart
"The Beast," by Donald Peart
Son of Man Prophesy Against the false prophet, by Donald Peart
The Dragon's Tail, Prophets who Teaches Lies, by Donald Peart
The Work of Lawlessness Revealed, by Donald Peart
When the Lord Made the Tempter, by Donald Peart
Examining Doctrine, Volume 1, by Donald Peart
Exousia, Your God Given Authority, by Donald Peart
The Numbers of God, by Donald Peart
The Completions of the Ages ... by Donald Peart
The Revelation of Jesus Christ, by Donald Peart
Jude—Translation and Commentary, by Donald Peart
Obtaining the Better Resurrection, by Donald Peart
Manifestations from Our Lord Jesus ...by Donald and Judith Peart
The New Testament, Dr. Donald Peart Exegesis
Dr. Donald Peart New Testament Exegesis II (without footnotes)
The Tree of Life, By Dr. Donald Peart
The Spirit and Power of John, the Baptist by Dr. Donald Peart
Is She Married to a Husband? by Donald Peart

The Ugliest Man God Made by Donald Peart
Does Answering the Call of God Impact Your Children? by Donald Peart
Victory Out of the Beast-the Harvest of the Earth by Donald Peart
Melchizedek by Donald Peart
Ezekiel-the House-the City-the Land (Interpreting the Patterns) by Donald Peart
Butter and Honey (Understanding How to Choose the Good and Refuse Evil), by Donald Peart
Wholly Maturing and Wholly Inheriting, Spirit, Soul, and Body, by Donald Peart
Angels and the Supernatural, by Donald Peart
The Prophetic Patterns of the Two Witnesses, by Donald Peart
Born a Second Time (Spirit with the Spirit), by Donald Peart
The Sweet Incense of Prayer by Donald Peart
Her Seed vs his Seed (Outlined Notes by Donald Peart)
Melchizedek Order, the Matured Priesthood (Outlined Notes by Donald Peart)

All books are available in Kindle eBook format.

CONTACT INFORMATION

Crown of Glory Ministries
P.O. Box 1041 Randallstown, MD 21133
donaldpeart7@gmail.com

ABOUT THE AUTHOR:

Donald Peart has been married to Judith Peart since 1986. They believe that Jesus is the Christ, the Son of the living God; and they preach the gospel of God's kingdom centered on Jesus Christ. They have founded and currently oversee Crown of Glory Ministries in Randallstown, Maryland. Donald and his wife have written over 45 books; and their ministry has distributed their books both in America and abroad. Donald has earned an Associate of Arts degree in Pre-Engineering, and a Bachelor of Science degree in Civil Engineering. a Master of Science in Construction Management, and a Doctorate in Theology.